Finding My Way To Freedom

Dr. Thomas Karl Reiner
With Joel Mark Harris

Cover Design by: Dennis Deauna

Finding My Way To Freedom is a work of nonfiction. Nonetheless some names and persons characteristics of individuals or events have been changed to disguise their identity. Resulting resemblance to persons living or dead is entirely coincidental and unintentional.

The publication is designed to provide accurate information regarding the subject matter covered. It is sold with the understanding that the publisher and author is not engaged in rendering legal, accounting, or other professional services. If legal advice or other expert assistance is required the service of a competent professional person should be sought.

Thomas Karl Reiner, author, *Finding My Way To Freedom* ©*2018*

ISBN-13: 978-1984198105

ISBN-10: 1984198106

Published in the United States

Table of Contents

Foreword

by Tami Peavy

Many years ago, Tom Reiner walked into one of my physical therapy clinics as a patient, after having shoulder surgery. With his Hungarian accent, his educated gentleman's manner and a clever sense of humor, it was simply impossible not be intrigued by this man. He clearly had experienced a very interesting life to this point. As his Physical Therapist, I saw he pushed himself quite hard in therapy so he could return as quickly as possible to playing tennis. Among all my patients over the years, Tom was, without a doubt, the most active man his age I had ever met.

As I got to know Tom, I discovered the key to his energy and vigor for life comes from his minds perspective on life as well as sheer determination. I learned he had lived through the brutalities of Russian Communism, German occupation, the Holocaust, civil war, revolution, personal loss and deep human suffering that would send most of us into a lifetime of psychological counseling. But through it all, he taught himself to focus not on the struggles and problems, but on problem-solving and possible solutions. He put his engineering mind to work to see past emotions of fear and even desperation. He concentrated instead on creating alternatives and then predicting the outcomes with various scenarios. This process kept him from panic and fear. Like turning a Rubik's Cube over and over from one combination to another to solve the puzzle.

What is really remarkable about Tom, however, is through all the personal injustices and loss, the human cruelty he endured, his trials, and tribulations, Tom kept his humanity. Even though he has personally witnessed the absolute worst in people, he still always assumes the best in people.

Over the years, Tom has become a cherished close friend and mentor. We have worked on business deals, inventions, product designs and countless projects together. In working with Tom on various projects and business endeavors, I learned from him some important ways of thinking that made me a better business woman. He would tell me to 'work the problem' and avoid 'working the emotion" when it came to business. Many times, he told me, "if you put your energy into solutions and avoid being clouded by your personal emotions, you will make much more effective decisions". Countless times I saw him put this philosophy into action in negotiations. Few of us master that skill in our lifetimes.

Tom's story is a unique and complex one. It has twists and turns, full of adversity and human suffering; and yet splattered with colorful triumphs at every corner. I felt personally compelled to get his story into print. Now, after three years of work helping him format and write his memoirs, I am honored to be writing this foreword and be the one to bring Tom's story to you.

With my Physical Therapist and friend, Tami Peavy, MBA, MPT

Chapter 1:

My Early Years

For the casual observer, in the modern world, it may seem strange what I considered a normal childhood.

I was born in Budapest, Hungary on December 29th 1931. It was a dark time for Hungary and Europe in general. Life in Hungary was miserable, however as a child, I wasn't aware of the political situation going on around me. The economy was in crisis, foreign debt and inflation was skyrocketing. People were hungry and many farmers were having a hard time making ends meet.

Hitler was taking Germany by storm and would soon throw Europe into the worst chaos it had ever seen. But of course, I wasn't aware of any of that growing up. Everything seemed normal to me. As just a young kid, I didn't have a care in the world.

My family and I lived on the second floor of a brick apartment in a modest neighbourhood, Csengery Utca 39, when I was less than six-years-old. As a young boy, I contracted many childhood diseases including scarlet fever and mumps. I even had two illnesses at the same time, one was whooping cough, but I don't remember the other one. It was bad, whatever it was.

Health problems were a reality of most children during that period. My poor mother, Keller Jozsa, always sat next to my bed and kept a close eye on me. Every time I woke up she was there.

My mother was a very slender and beautiful woman, however, by the time I was six years old she was quite heavy. I don't have many memories from back then but I remember hearing she might have aborted a child. I have considered that could be why she put on the weight.

My mother Keller Jozsa. (Jozsa) She was born in 1895.

It wasn't customary to talk about personal things back then. In thinking back, perhaps the stress of my illness and the abortion took a toll on her. I can't know for sure. In any case I suppose that was the reason I was her only child.

Csengery Utca is a street on the east side of Budapest. Our street was filled with many tall brick buildings attached to each other and built in different styles so the front entrances were varying and distinguishable. This was common in Hungary at that time. The streets were made of cobblestone and there was no grass or trees on our street.

Our building was centrally located so it was easy to get around the city. There was this beautiful courtyard which we would sometimes play in. There was no privacy for myself or my parents. Our apartment consisted of one room heated by a central stove which we would burn wood or coal.

When I was five or six, my friends and I often played together. I ended up having a life-long friendship with five kids from elementary school: Peter Grosz, Tamas Kemeny, Robert Schultz, Frici Lorant and Berci Szanto.

Probably my best friend was Peter. We stayed friends for many years, through thick and thin. We played together, studied together, and worked together. His mother, Mucika, and sister Georgette were almost part of my family.

As kids, we frequently ran around on wooden scooters in the Erzsebet Ter, a small park in downtown Budapest. It was only a few blocks from the Danube River and was surrounded by tall buildings.

Budapest is actually two cities, Buda and Pest. Buda is the mountainous region, on the east bank. In the mountains, there is still the old king's castle. Pest is on the west bank. It is a flat area and a very busy city. The city united in 1873.

Back then there was a coffee shop at one side of the park where mothers could sit to watch their children play as we chased each other around the park. I often fell, scraping the skin off my knee many times.

The doctor warned me to stay off my scooter for awhile or I would have permanent scars. As a boisterous kid, I didn't care about scars, but my mother did and told me to be more careful, otherwise, she would always worry about me. For awhile I tried to be more careful, but getting into trouble was too much fun.

My friends and I were too young to know what was happening beyond our neighborhood. Hitler was closing in and soon the war would be at our doorstep. I was having fun like any child my age.

I have few memories from elementary school, which had only grades one to four. I vividly remember having a pretty woman as a teacher. Whenever a student got out of line, the teacher used a cane to slap the student's, extended right palm. I must have behaved reasonably well because she only punished me once. I don't remember what the punishment was for, but I remember it burned. That whole class was one big blur. I don't remember learning a single thing because I was so distracted by my teacher's beauty.

For my sixth birthday, my godfather gave me a large erector set made by the well-regarded German toy manufacturer, Marklin. I liked it a lot and it probably was what made me want to grow up to be an engineer. It was a career path I never wavered from. I made all kind of machines from the toy parts. I built a crane, which crawled around lifting items from the floor to help my mother clean up the apartment.

I had a friend, around this time, who lived a few doors away from our apartment house. As we grew older, we liked playing tricks on people. My friends and I would stand around looking at the roof of the building pretending to stare at something interesting. We would get people to look also which made us laugh. Then we would walk away and watched as people tried to guess what was happening on the roof. It was a very fun, cheap form of entertainment.

One day, we decided to build a pipe bomb. We filled the hollow shaft of a large key with water, plugged it up and threw it into the fire in a large ceramic tiled furnace, which was heating my friend's living room. We expected a loud noise – that was all. Instead, the pipe bomb blew the entire furnace apart. When my friend's father got home and saw the damage, we really got it. It turned out to be really expensive to fix. I guess we should have stuck with our rooftop joke.

Then there was a coffee shop on Andrassi ut, the Main Street of Budapest, where we went often. We would steal silverware and put it in our pockets until the waiters caught on what we were doing. After awhile, the staff asked us to do a handstand before we left to ensure we didn't take anything that didn't belong to us.

Though I had a curious mind and *did* love to learn, I did not do too well in high school in the first and second grade.

My parents bought an encyclopedia set. I will never forget that it had 20 volumes: 18 were original information and two were supplemental updates. I read that encyclopedia from A to Z, more times than I can recall. I can tell you that the first book went from A to Bad, the second went from Bad to Bur, the third went from Bur to Don, the fourth from Don to Fel, the next one ended at Goz, then

Hit, Jos, Kob, then Man. That is all I can remember, but keep in mind I got that set and studied it over 76 years ago!

My lack of academic success prompted my parents to find a tutor for me. They found a boy named Vamos Bandi, who was only a little bit older than me. Vamos was about 15-years-old and must have helped me a lot, because I never had problems at school after he started working with me. We liked each other and very quickly became friends. I met many of his friends and was no longer bored at school. I looked forward to the tutoring sessions so Vamos could help me with my lessons. Associating with boys three to four years older than me was a very good influence.

Vamos and his friends had a club where they met every week. I was allowed to attend the meetings, which made me very proud. They regularly voted on different topics; it was a very democratic group. The voting was done by hand, and each member would write their vote on a piece of paper. Then the votes had to be tallied by hand. The process was very cumbersome.

Inspired by my favorite toy, I decided to automate the voting process. Using the parts from my erector set, I built a vote-counting machine. By creating a large knob that rotated with each vote, at the end of process, the members of the society knew immediately which idea had the most votes, signifying a win. The machine was a success and the older boys elected me as a member of their society, which was quite an honor for me!

*　　　*　　　*　　　*

When children were not in school, it was customary for middle-income families to escape the heat of summer in the city by spending July and August in a rented country home. A favorite destination was Lake Balaton, which is southwest of Budapest and is

Hungary's largest freshwater lake. It was a very popular place for Hungarians to enjoy recreational activities. My family frequently went there. Traditionally, mothers took their children to the lake in the country and fathers joined them on the weekend, commuting to the city to work during the week. Our family did just that.

One summer, when I was maybe five years old, mother and I rented a room at the farmer's cottage up in the Carpatian Mountains in northeast Hungary. The farmer there had a daughter who was a couple of years older than me, who I played with. We had a good time.

One day her mother said that she needed mushrooms, to make an omelet. Her daughter and I had to go into the woods and pick the mushrooms. As we were collecting them on one side of some bushes, I looked up and on the other side was a bear standing on his back feet eating the berries. I stood there frozen for a moment. It wasn't a big bear, not much bigger than a golden retriever. The bear then looked at me for half a second. I don't know who got more scared – me or the bear – the bear and I ran in opposite directions!

One summer at Lake Balaton, I don't remember how old I was, maybe seven, mother made fried chicken and a potato dish that Americans would call French fries. We had it for dinner and I loved it so much my mother prepared it the next day too. On the third day of our stay in the country, mother asked me what I would like for dinner. Naturally I answered 'fried chicken with French fries. To my surprise, she made it again. After several days of me wanting the same dinner, mother got angry because all I asked for was 'fried chicken and French fries'.

She said 'I will make nothing but fried chicken and French fries until you get so tired of them, Tomi, that you will not want to look at them anymore!'

I ate nothing but fried chicken and French fries that *entire* summer. It might not have been a balanced diet, but I didn't care because it tasted good and I was happy.

My Apu, my father (a nickname popular in Hungary) visited the lake house over the weekend. He liked to go bottom fishing in

Lake Balaton, his favorite summer activity. He would put weights on his line, add whatever bait he happened to have onto the hook, and then drop it to the bottom of the lake where he let it sit overnight.

One day my father was very eager to fish after a long and tiring week at work. I watched him set everything up just so, but he caught nothing all day. I felt very badly for him, so that night I went to the lake with my cousin and filled his hooks with sardines and gefilte fish which is made from a mixture of different kinds of white fish. You can imagine how surprised he was the next morning when he pulled the hooks out of the water full of canned fish!

My father was the manager and did the accounting for a prominent yard good store downtown called *Szenasi Hoffman es Tarsa*. It was the largest goods store in Budapest. During this period of time, there were no ready-made suits available. Anybody who wanted new clothes went to a tailor who had catalogs full of styles to inspire style selection, and swatches of material to pick color. Once the material for a dress or suit was selected, the tailor bought the material from a yard goods store and then would sew the suit or dress for his client. Frequently, the material was bought from Szenasi.

Father was also a minor partner in the store. The majority owner, Szenasi, who was my father's closest friend, became my godfather when later we joined the Reformed Church. We were Jewish, but we found people of our faith were rapidly finding themselves to be out of favor with the government.

My mother had a sister in Vienna whose family was exterminated after the Anschluss (political joining of Austria and Germany after Hitler's rise to power).

My cousin Gyuri (George) Reiner who died on the death march through the Carpathian Mountains on the way to Berchtesgaden Extermination Camp

Many of my family members died during that time period. I don't have many details beyond the knowledge that they all died either from death marches or in the extermination camps.

My family was not religious. I never learned Hebrew, the Talmud or much about the Jewish faith in school, so joining Szenasi at his church seemed like a good idea to protect us from anti-Semitism and hopefully from the Holocaust.

Szenasi, had a girlfriend on the side. Her name was Ica Keszler. She was very nice and eventually took an interest in my father. They started having an affair and I heard arguments between my parents about many things, especially about Ica, but divorce was never considered an option.

None of us knew it at the time, but Ica would play a vital part in our survival.

Chapter 2:

Invasion

In 1943, we were living in an apartment on the third floor of Kiraly Utca 97. At that time, my father decided to have the walls painted and decorated. That was a big event for us and I was excited. It took weeks to move the furniture, paint the walls, then decorate them with scrolls and move the furniture back.

That year, instead of going to the country, we went to the Grand Hotel on Margit Sziget, an island on the Danube at Budapest. That was an excellent and expensive hotel. My father took a room for us for a week. We liked it so much we stayed another week, but because the hotel was booked, we had to move to another room. That went on for a month – we kept moving from one room to another weekly.

The Regent of Hungary, Miklos Horty, a former admiral and statesman, was staying there at that time. The monarchy had been overthrown and Horty had returned from exile with the National Army to form government, so he was the de facto head of state at that time.

He dined at 2 p. m, which was customary. One could choose to eat at his table or eat before or after him. We usually ate at the far end of his table, which meant we had to abide by the etiquette. Because I was a teenager, there was a waiter assigned to me to teach me the etiquette of eating. We had to place down the utensils when the Regent spoke. We had to end eating a dish when he was finished with it. We could only talk, when he was not talking, and had to keep our voices low, talking only to people next to us. Naturally, the Regent was very attentive to everybody. He pretended to continue eating a serving until it seemed everybody was finished with it, which we signaled by placing our forks and knives parallel on the dish.

Nothing could be touched by hand. Even an apple had to be held down by a fork and peeled by a knife. The peeled apple had to be then cut into small segments and eaten one segment at a time. It was considered impolite to bend forward to eat above the dish, talk with food in one's mouth or put a large piece of food into one's mouth. Taking anything out of one's mouth was out of question, which made everybody careful of putting strange or even doubtful food into one's mouth. It was tedious and complex procedure. On days Horty had a lot to say, we ate cold food or very little food.

*   *   *   *

One of the royal officials, who staying at the hotel, had a BMW 128 sport car – an open two-seater. It was a beautiful shiny car and today would be a collector's dream. One of his servants was entrusted with taking care of the car. I made friends with the servant and he allowed me to drive it. It was my first time behind the wheel.

We only went 5 or 10 kilometers an hour, however, and I was over-correcting with the steering wheel, like most first-time drivers. My feet could barely reach the pedals. Afterwards I was very excited to learn more about driving and would eventually own many amazing vehicles. As I got older, driving and cars would be a large part of my life.

At the hotel, there was a large outdoor swimming pool attached to the main building. In fact, both the hotel and the swimming pool are there even today. At one end of the pool, a natural hot spring fed warm water into the pool. That part was shallow and was partially covered. Even during the snowy, winter days, the warm end of the pool is comfortable.

One Sunday morning we were staying there, father excitedly explained to us that Regent Horty decided to invite the Americans to occupy Hungary after Hitler was putting extreme pressure on him to turn his country more towards fascism.

Regent Horty went on the radio and announced that everybody should stay calm, American parachuters would be dropping from airplanes and advised everybody the government had invited the Americans.

Instead of the parachuters, we soon saw the German troops arriving on motorcycles with sidecars, armored vehicles and tanks. They entered Hungary through the main road without any opposition.

Later, we learned that one of Regent Horty's assistant was planted there by Hitler and that he had forewarned the Nazis of Horty's plans. The German army stationed at the border was ready to invade Hungary at a moment's notice and did so when Hitler learned of the upcoming parachute drop. The German army swept in without any opposition and the American's parachute drop was cancelled.

I didn't know what to make of the new invaders. I do remember my parents were very concerned and would whisper quietly amongst themselves. The Germans posted large posters on all the doors, instigating a 9 pm curfew and forced all the Jews to move to the ghettos. It took awhile to get used to the German occupation and seeing German soldiers everywhere.

During the war, there was very a strong anti-Semitic feeling everywhere, even in school. My father was heavily decorated in 1919 for fighting against the Russian communists who tried to overtake Hungary. Because of his efforts, we were treated less severely than most Jews. My father wanted to save our family from the horror being experienced by other European Jews. First, he applied for us to immigrate to the Netherlands. When that failed, he decided to change our religion to Reformed.

The Reformed religion was a minority in Hungary. It was Christian-based without the complex rituals and graven images that were so common in other Christian churches. Religious education was compulsory. Catholicism was the state religion and the main religion taught at school. Students had to receive permission to be excused from those classes to study their own religion. I went to the Reformed studies as long as possible.

Jewish children were routinely abused by the other students with the approval of the teachers. The teacher would make Jewish students grab their ankles, then the rest of the class would line up and kick them in the arse, one after the other. Not having to attend Jewish religious classes kept me from having to endure some of the abuse.

Around 1943 or so, the situation in Hungary got worse. Instead of joining the Boy Scouts, the children had to join the Hungarian equivalent of a 'Hitler Jugend' organization, a Nazi group for kids. Naturally, Jewish kids were not allowed in the organization. Instead, we were organized into work brigades and were taught to pick up the mines from the railroads. I was made a group leader, because my father was decorated in 1919 for fighting against the communists. I even had a pistol which I wore on my belt.

I wore a white band on my arm instead of a yellow star on my chest. Our mission was to remove land mines laid on the tracks by the Hungarian resistance. However, we were careful to leave every second mine on the rails. That act of defiance was our small, youthful contribution against the Nazis.

The situation for Jews got gradually worse and worse after the invasion. Even before the German invasion, most of the Jews were either living in the ghetto or were forced to move there. Eventually the Jews were crammed into railroad cattle cars and taken to death camps such as Auschwitz.

There they were forced into slave labor or exterminated. Many horrendous experiments were performed on them. They were submerged into ice cold water until they froze, boiled in extreme heat, had their hair plucked from their bodies, among other terrible tortures until eventually they were killed. They were usually herded into showers, where poison gas was fed through the shower heads instead of water. Every useful part of their body was processed and anything of value was taken from them.

Around this time, my father was called into the army. Because of his war medals, he was put in charge of a Jewish labor camp. The Coronel, who was my dad's commanding officer, was a Nazi and would torture the Jews by brutally beating them and hanging them up by the hands behind their backs.

My dad didn't want to be part of this, ditched his uniform, and went AWOL. He managed to sneak home and hide from the Nazis. For months, he sat on a chair behind the counter at Szenasi store with my mother, not even daring to sneeze.

My father's mistress, Ica Keszler, found an abandoned painter's shack, helped dig a large pit under the ground floor, and placed a chair for my father to sit there. Ica took food to father daily for months to keep him alive.

Ica also gave her birth certificate to my mother and her nephew's birth certificate to me. My mother became Josepha Keszler and I became Anthony Keszler. We pretended that we were refugees from the Eastern Front, fleeing from the advancing Russian troops and were registered as such. The Administrator for refugees gave us a room at an apartment in a building that was previously a whorehouse.

This was a very brave act on part of Ica, who risked her life daily to keep us alive. My mother, in turn, had to face a grave moral dilemma: the same woman, who was her husband's lover, saved the lives of the whole family, with no demands on any of us.

Those were very difficult times in the world and for my family. Now I know that we were very lucky that Ica came into our lives. She put forth a significant effort to hide and protect the three of us. She must have really loved my father because she put her own life in danger, risking torture and execution. Horrible things happened to people who helped the Jews.

Thankfully, Ica survived the war and fell in love with a CIA operative who worked at the American consulate. They got married and after the consulate closed they moved to Washington D.C. Many years later, I would go visit them and thank Ica for saving my family.

Chapter 3:

The Siege of Budapest

L ate in 1944, Russian soldiers surrounded Budapest, trapping the German and Hungarian soldiers in the city. Hitler ordered his army to defend the city to the last man, while Stalin ordered Budapest to be taken without canons. In total, including citizens, over 100,000 people would be killed in the battle for Budapest.

I had just turned 13 years old. With constant gunfire, the smoke, fire from bombs, and the smell of death all around, it would be the worst part of the war for our family. The entire city was in chaos. Everybody who could leave did, escaping the fighting. The rest of us lived in misery as constant fear of death.

The Soviet advance was slow and brutal, going from building to building, rooting out the Germans. Ambushes were set up in the sewers which were used as troop movement. Thousands of casualties mounted on both sides.

My mother and I moved down to the coal cellar, where each apartment had a storage cubicle. It was dark and damp down there. The cubicles were infested with rats and mice. We could hear their tiny feet constantly scuttle day and night. It was dreadful, but the alternative was to risk being found by the Nazis. We slept there for months on top of the coal and chopped wooden logs. We lost contact with everybody during this time. I often thought about Peter and my other friends, wondering if they were even still alive.

To pass the time, I played cards with my mother by the candle light we had made. Mother taught me to tear a shirt into strips that we rolled tightly to be used as a wick. I then made the wax out of pork fat and rolled them into small candles. Making candles wasn't hard. The tedious work filled our time and it was easy to be silent as we worked.

At one point, we heard Russian soldiers above. They had taken over the third floor of our building and were fighting the Germans who occupied the ground floor. We could hear the shouting and the gun fighting from below, praying the building wouldn't collapse or that they would find us.

Food was always hard to come by and I would have to go scavenge for it. I found a large sack of dried beans somewhere which kept us going for a long time. We soaked the beans in any water we could find and ate them cold. They tasted awful but there was little we could do about it. We couldn't cook them well in our situation. The beans were hard and tasteless. I vowed if I made it out alive, I would never eat beans again.

On another one of my trips outside, I found a dead horse under a snow pile by the side of the road. I took out a knife and carved out pieces of meat from the carcass before covering it back again with snow, hoping nobody else would find it. Thankfully the snow preserved it somewhat.

If I thought hard, semi-cooked beans tasted bad, I wasn't prepared for horse meat. We cooked pieces of horse meat on our small homemade candles and eat it as best as we could. It was very tough and kind of sweet, believe it or not. We managed to ration the horsemeat for about a month before it ran out.

In addition to food, I would always scout for fresh water which was in short supply. Once I found an abandoned wine cellar. Someone had punched holes in a few barrels and I could smell the fermented grapes. The cellar floor was covered knee-deep in wine. After I collected most of the vine from that cellar I found two dead soldiers at the bottom. They had probably been the ones who had punctured the holes. For weeks, I would carry a bucket of wine back to our cellar hideout.

Eventually my father thought it was safe enough to join us from the painter's shack he had been hiding in. My father decided our hiding spot was a little too dangerous and took us to a new location. My only living grandparent, my mother's mother, was hiding nearby. My father and I decided to get her and bring her back with us. We knew it was risky and we might get discovered. My father, of course, didn't have any documentation and without it the Germans would likely execute us.

We snuck out of the cellar, but we didn't make it far before we heard a voice commanding us to stop. My father and I stood still, barely moving, our arms stiff. A Hungarian Nazi soldier was standing there, clutching his gun. He asked for my father's papers. I could see my Father struggling to figure out what to do. The Nazi's eyes darted briefly towards me but then fixated back on my Father.

Thankfully, I still had the pistol from my time as a youth brigade. The soldier was still staring at my father. I knew if I didn't act, he would kill us both. We didn't even count as citizens. We were worse than rodents. I knew what I had to do; my breathing was calm. I pulled out the pistol and shot the soldier. The gun made a loud cracking sound, the soldier collapsed. We took a step closer to examine him but he was dead.

Much later, people would ask me if I was scared, faced with such a choice. My attitude is that emotions – like panic, fear, or sadness – don't help in those situations. It impairs your thinking and causes you to say or do something stupid.

We left the dead solider and collected my grandmother, praying nobody would stop us on the way back. Luckily our return trip was without incident.

Life was a constant struggle. There was very little water trickling from the faucets at ground level because the power plants were damaged and there was no fuel to operate them. We kept a pan under the faucet to catch any drips. The water was our most precious resource and we didn't waste a drop to it.

We soon ate all the fried goose liver Grandma had preserved. She had been smart and had started to stockpile food months before the Russians invaded. We were thankful for her foresight because without her, we might have starved. But even with her rations, we eventually ran out of food, so out of necessity I risked going back up from the cellar in search of sustenance. I would find bits of scrap food here and there that would last us until the end of the war.

After 'liberation' by Russian soldiers, we went back to the apartment home at Kiraly Utca 97, the three-story apartment house where we lived before going into hiding. The apartment was still there, but the outside wall had been demolished by a 500 Kg bomb dropped during a rare visit by an American B29. Though the apartment was missing an outside wall, we had a bigger problem – there was no food to eat in the city. We effectively covered the hole in the wall by hanging a heavy rug over it, but finding food was a more difficult problem to resolve.

My mother offered to pawn the last item of value she owned, a ring. My father, my cousin Zsuzsi, and I walked many kilometers to the countryside where we traded the gold ring for a loaf of bread and some potatoes. It was exhausting work.

While carrying our booty home, we came across a locomotive pushing a railroad car to test for mines on the rails. The locomotive would hit an empty wagon, making it roll forward and explode any rail mines on impact. It was quite a process. After the explosions were set off and the damaged rails repaired, the wagon was righted onto the tracks and the process was repeated. We were allowed to stand on the side rail of the locomotive and held on tight, hoping not to fall off or get blown up. It beat walking with all the food we had.

*　　*　　*　　*

It was February and Budapest had been turned to rubble. The streets were littered with debris and dead bodies everywhere. The entire city reeked of decay and rot. We were afraid with Spring coming, the snow would melt, and the rotting remains would start a disease epidemic. We only had until April before the snow melted so my father and I fashioned a sled out of the box spring of a bed and used it to carry dead bodies to the cemetery. It took us 6 weeks to bury all the bodies. It was a very grueling process but by that time death was so common place that dragging corpses around didn't bother me.

We each used an old pair of gloves that were for skiing. It was a very hard job to dig graves in the frozen ground with pick axes, but it had to be done. When we ran out of room in the cemetery we buried the bodies in the nearby square in Kiraly Utca, where my friends and I used to play when we were small. I do not know if the bodies were ever moved since we buried them in 1945. By the time spring came and the snow melted, all dead bodies were underground so we had successfully avoided disease.

After things started to return to normal, my father took over Szenasi's downtown Budapest yard good store. His friend, my godfather Szenazi, no longer wanted any part of it. The store was quite successful, but the building was confiscated by the Russian government from a Germany company as war retribution and demanded that father pay his rent in gold.

Hungarian currency had the value of toilet paper at that time so the Russians didn't want payment in our devalued currency, favouring gold instead, even though it was not legal tender under communist rule. Father had to buy gold on the black market just to pay rent.

During the time that my father ran Szenasi's, we had a three-bedroom apartment on the 3rd floor of Vaci Utca 3, which was a main street, downtown. We also had a servant who stayed with us, too. Back then having hot water required going downstairs, getting coal and wood, then bringing it upstairs to put in the water heater, which was in the bathroom. Then you had to start the fire and – hopefully – there was warm water ready for your bath later on.

Despite some of the hardships, Szenasi's was profitable and we were able to save some money and could afford a live-in maid. She was pretty and I was instantly attracted to her. She got up very early to prepare the hot water for us. Having hot water was a big luxury that most other families couldn't afford.

One day while my father and mother were gone, the live-in maid and I decided to experiment with each other a little. I felt a mixture of excitement and nervousness as I ran my fingers across her body. She was very shy as we fumbled along, not knowing what we were doing.

My poor father came home unexpectedly and found the maid and I half undressed. You need to understand that at the time I did not know a single 16-year-old virgin in Hungary, they just didn't seem to exist. I had just turned 17 and messing around was common, but that was the only time I can remember my father losing his temper.

He lectured me right in the downtown square where the shop was and told me that I should not have sex with anybody, because that is not right and I didn't have any idea what problems it could get me into.

I pretended not to understand what he said, because he was not being specific. Father would never say sex or make any specific comments. He just talked around and around the issue. I just looked at him making funny faces, acting confused, playing games with him and pretending I did not understand.

He finally gave up and said "Oh, just go fuck her!" We were still out in the square and people around us could hear us. That was the only time I heard my father get upset and use that kind of language. He was a very proper gentleman and I was his only child

My dad worked at Szenasi's from 1945 to 1948, until it didn't make economic sense anymore to keep the business going because the rent was too steep. Inflation made converting Hungarian currency to gold too expensive and ate into all the profits. My dad sold everything in the store and closed it down. After, he had no job for almost two years.

Finally, late in 1949, my father found a job at a race track. Horse racing was very popular in Hungary. Computers did not exist then and betting was an important part of the race. Someone had to calculate the odds for the betters and my father could add numbers fast, so he was hired. He had to calculate the odds continuously for every race. A helper would hold up and display the result of his calculation, so the betters could make their decisions.

We struggled for money during this time, so my mother also got a job as a bookkeeper. I don't remember where she worked, but I do remember that she got a job to help the family. We were so poor that sometimes we had nothing to eat. I remember Christmas of 1950, we were very hungry and my father sold his overcoat so we could buy food – it was freezing cold outside. That was just one of many such experiences, but we stuck together and didn't give up.

In 1952, my father got a job at the Ministry of Agriculture as an accountant and gradually got promoted to the position of Chief Auditor. By then things started to look up for us as a family. However, Hungary still was a disaster.

Chapter 4:

My School Years

I entered gymnasium, where students prepared to enter university when I was ten years old. The school had been interrupted for one year during 1945 when the gymnasium closed down because the fighting was too intense. It reopened in August of 1946.

I would go to gymnasium for eight to ten hours, six days a week. We had one large exercise room, where we had occasional gymnastics, basketball, fencing and other activities after the day's lectures. We attended for eight years, unless we failed a year and had to repeat it. If that was the case, gymnasium could last nine to ten years. The benefit of that grueling schedule was that we got very good education, though not necessarily an easy one.

I must say that when my own children reached this age in America, I was very troubled by the schools they attended. Their education was not like my schooling in Hungary. To me, it seems that the standards are lower here in the U.S. in an effort to make sure that everybody graduates. I appreciated my struggles in my Hungarian schools. I really had to learn the lessons to pass on to the next class.

When I was growing up, Hungarian high schools offered students two different choices. The first option was called "gymnasium" which is, similar to what the English call a "Prep School".

Gymnasium, the Hungarian high school which I attended for 8 years.

This gymnasium was not like a Roman gymnasium where students constantly trained, although exercise was part of the overall program. Basketball was a very popular sport which I played quite often. I was very active and enjoyed learning, too. I learned to like school thanks to Vamos' tutoring.

The other choice was the "polgari" which was for those who wanted to learn a trade instead of having to learn Latin and mathematics. Polgari students wore a green beret, so it was easy to spot them. They liked to start fights and beat us up. My friend Peter and I got into many fights. I learned quickly to never back down, to find the most aggressive polgari student in the group and beat him up first. The others would run away when they saw us do that. Fighting was entertaining and taught us to stand up to a challenge.

Because I wanted to be an engineer, I chose gymnasium, but I had the opportunity to try classes offered at polgari as well. It was not the same the other way around: polgari students could not attend classes at gymnasium. As a gymnasium student I had to work harder, but I also had more options upon graduation.

My mother enrolled me, but she seldom visited the school. I have no idea what occupied her days after I started school.

We were told by the teachers that anybody who wanted to smoke could, but only in a designated room to avoid burning the building down. Out of the 42 students in my class, divided into two segments, only two continued to smoke. They were older than the rest of us, because they were repeating classes. I always found it interesting that none of my close friends ever smoked. We were exposed to smokers, both of my parents smoked and so did my cousin. I knew a few kids who smoked back in those days. I saw one of my old classmates a few years ago and he is still smoking. That is interesting to me, since smoking is so unhealthy. With everything that we experienced growing up, he is still alive *and* smoking.

The first work projects I took on when I was in high school was repairing bicycle wheels by straightening bent rims. I took the front fork off the bicycle and nailed it to the kitchen table, sticking out horizontally parallel to the floor. I placed a wheel into the fork and by tightening and loosening the spokes, the rims straightened out. My mother didn't like this as it made holes in her table, but it allowed me to make pocket money, so she didn't stop me.

Since the bicycle repair was going well, I got ambitious and decided to build a complete bicycle. I convinced my German teacher to buy it from me and advance the money for material. I built the bicycle for him, but at that time I did not know that the frame had to be a parallelogram. One day the German teacher drove his bicycle off the sidewalk and the front tube of the frame, which held the handle bars to the wheel, broke. My design was not a parallelogram and therefore could not distribute the weight under stress properly. That was my first real life example of stress points and weight distribution, something that I would become quite an expert in.

When I was 17-years-old

During those school years, we usually went dancing on Saturday nights at a local dance hall. We danced waltzes, polka, jitterbug, tango, and other popular dances of the period. Cutting in was not allowed, but it happened frequently. The disputes that followed someone cutting in were usually settled by a fight and those fights were the height of the entertainment. Everybody joined in, even those who did not know what the fight was about. It made for fun times and everyone enjoyed the excitement of the battle. Knives were not allowed, and anybody who pulled a knife was jumped by anyone who was near.

Fighting was a popular way to use our youthful energy, especially after the war. There was a boy in our class that we called Butyok. That is a Turkish word that means *callus*, like the calluses on your feet. I don't remember why we called him that, but we did. We all liked to jump that poor guy and beat him up.

It was during this same time in my life that I became very fond of Opera. The Hungarian State Opera House was only few blocks from our home on Madach Imre ut.

The Opera House is a three-story tribute to 19th century Hungarian architecture, made of bricks with columns, arches and many statues. It is a beautiful building. Inside it is even grander than it is outside with plush red velvet seating, a beautiful chandelier and artwork on the ceiling. Everything was made of beautifully hand carved wood. I went to the opera three or four times a week for years. One of my friend's wife was a ballet dancer. My Father liked opera, too. His favorite opera was Traviata.

I remember many situations where things didn't go quite right. One time a singer from Yugoslavia, was the lead in Faust, Mephisto. If you remember the story, Faust sells his soul to the devil, Mephisto, for youth, knowledge, and power. He falls in love with Marguerite and their love is both passionate and tragic.

The Yugoslavian singer was late and did not have his costume due to problems with his train ride. He had to wear a costume that was available at the Budapest Opera House, which didn't quite fit his large belly. There were several scenes in that opera with special effects. One involved wine coming out of a barrel which hung in front of the tavern. After the Yugoslavian sung, he was supposed to tap the barrel and the wine (water really) would start to flow. However, unfortunately, the wine didn't come out. The Yugoslavian kept singing and tapping and looking desperately at the conductor who whispered: "What the hell can we do?" Just as the conductor spoke, the barrel burst and poured water all over the poor actor, soaking him.

In another scene, Faust has a sword. He swishes it in a circle and sparks fly. That is usually accomplished by sandpaper on the floor creating sparks as Mephisto runs the tip of his sword over it. That year, they decided to modernize the set and made Mephisto to use a sword connected by a long wire to the electric power off the stage. As Mephisto swung his sword around on the stage the wires short circuited and all the lights went out in the Opera House!

One of the most exciting moments that I had at the Opera House was when a man was smoking a cigarette on the upper floor, where they stored the costumes. He threw his cigarette away and it landed on some of the costumes and started a fire. The sprinkler system came on, but it was focused on the grand hall downstairs, where the beautiful red velvet chairs were. Everybody watched in horror as the very expensive chairs got soaked, ruining them while meanwhile, the fire still raged on the upper floor. The fire department was also called and they came out, but the ladders weren't tall enough to get up to the level that was on fire, so they called for the only truck in the entire fire department with a high ladder. There was only one such ladder truck in existence at that time in Budapest.

The ladder truck came on the Korut, a main street that goes all around Budapest, but some guy ran his car out in the road in front of it. The ladder truck driver swerved to miss the car and it overturned.

The fire was still burning and the firemen had to do something to put it out, so a few of them started trying to climb the brick wall in front of the Opera House with a hose, hoping to get up to the windows and put out the fire. They soon realized that the water pump wasn't strong enough to shoot the water up that high, so they brought in a gas engine driven pump, which wouldn't start.

I was home hearing all of the commotion, so I ran over there just in time to see them trying to fix the gas engine to get it going. I stepped in and told them I could start it up for them. I examined the inside and thankfully was able to get it going so they were finally able to put out the fire. There was not a lot of damage to the building, except to the ground level seats, but a lot of the costumes were ruined.

My close friends and I liked to organize balls for all the students. There were no girls in our school, but we had a 'sister school' nearby. We brazenly left class one day, went to the sister school, and told the teacher there that we needed the help of some of the girls to organize the annual ball. The teachers allowed a few girls to join us.

We put together various performances of singing and short plays for the ball. We danced and drank whatever we could get our hands on. While the other students danced, my girlfriend and I sat behind a curtain on the stage. There we kissed and made out. She was escorted by her friend's mother, who eventually got worried when she could not see my girlfriend on the dance floor. She found the principal, who knew exactly where to find us: behind the curtain!

Our group of friends formed the English Club and got permission to use one of the rooms in the basement of the school for our meetings. In the room was an old armchair that served as a substitute bed. It was very convenient and a way to be with our girlfriends. That worked until somebody told the principal what was happening. Once our plans were discovered, we decided to take the armchair apart and smuggle it out in pieces.

We had an outstanding language teacher which we nicknamed 'Chocho'. He was a professor at the university until he was demoted to teach at a high school, because he spoke out against communism. He taught us Latin, English, Greek, German and whatever else that we were curious about.

He introduced a word by its origin, Sanskrit, Latin, or Greek or whatever it was. He then took us through its variations over the ages to its current use in different countries. Nobody could ever forget a word after such an interesting dissertation. He had great respect from everybody. He did not teach like the other teachers, he lectured like he had done at the University. He had our full attention and never had to ask for silence, nor did he have to discipline anybody. He was always dressed in a dark suit, blue and white striped shirt with a hard collar, cufflinks, bowler hat and an umbrella, rain or shine. You could hear a pin drop when he was teaching.

Our history teacher was a retired boxer. He was an absolute idiot, who knew nothing about history. He came in carrying a history book, slammed it down on his desk and read the page it opened up to. Soon we learned his procedure and creased his book at one place. It predictably opened there every time. We learned about prehistoric England for years and studied nothing else. I enjoy watching the History channel now so that I can learn so many things that I did not know due to my studies – or lack of studies, in school.

The principal, Regos, was a great man also. He had only one arm because he lost the other during World War I. Regos worked with us and we worked with him. One of my close friends and I installed an intercom system for the whole building. Regos would announce news over the intercom to all classes, which was unheard of at that time.

His wife was a little strange. She was always urging us to pee in our bath in order to have nice smooth skin all over our body. I had to try it, just to see. I still had lousy skin even after that crazy experiment.

We had a music teacher who we always gave a hard time to. When he wanted us to sing a song, we sang *"The Shit got Thrown Over the Fence"* no matter what song he requested. One day we took his chair and hung it out the window before he arrived. He could not sit down so he ran to the principal's office to complain. By the time he came back with the principal, the chair was back in place. We had a good laugh over that.

Another very good teacher was a woman who taught Physics and Pre-med. Like our English teacher, Chocho, the students respected and listened to her. She also had no discipline problems in class. When she presented something new, a boy would do the experiment to demonstrate what the teacher was talking about.

I still remember he taught us that aspirin is *acetylosalicylicum*, i.e. salicylic acid. Aspirin works by making your body acidic, so that it fights infection efficiently. Did you know that Alka Seltzer is also acetylosalicylicum with a little fizz in it? Fizzy or not, it is just acetylsalicylic acid.

The Chemistry teacher was a doctor. Many of our parents used him when they needed a doctor. Doctors did not have offices in Hungary. They just came to your house with their medical bag. This guy was very good, but he gave everybody an enema before starting the checkup. He was famous for that; enema was his specialty.

He told us a story about a time he was lecturing in university and he asked what the hardest part of the body was. A girl raised her hand and said, "the penis." Our class thought that was pretty funny. After telling the story, he gave us a lecture about how the penis gets hard.

At graduation, the school received an envelope from the government with examination questions. For mathematics, three students sat before a blackboard and one after the other had to solve a problem. My question was to derive the equation for calculating the volume of a sphere. After solving that problem, I helped the other two students solve their problems.

Although I didn't have the best education, looking back, I have no regrets about what I learned at school. After I graduated I had no problem finding work and when I went on to higher education, I was readily admitted. My grades were always exceptional.

*   *   *   *

I graduated to an engine-driven bicycle around 1947 when I was 16. You had to pedal hard to start the engine, which was able propel the bike slowly forward without pedaling. Soon I traded it for a real motorcycle, a Matra. Starting that motorcycle required you run and jump on it while it was in motion, get the wheels rolling then jump on it to start. It was a little faster and more fun than the motorized bicycle; however, I did not get permission from my father to trade motorcycles. As you might imagine, he got very angry. That occasion was the only time he hit me for doing something wrong.

The next vehicle I got was an NSU motorcycle. The company, Neckarsulm Strickmaschinen Union was headquartered in the southern German town of Neckarsulm. It was a real motorcycle, but it still had to be started by pedaling first. Mobility was important to me; I could go farther and much faster than walking.

My mother got me a summer job as an apprentice to an electrician. We were wiring a concrete army barrack. The contractor placed a one-inch-square lumber in the wall where the conduits were to be installed later. The wood would create a channel of sorts in the concrete walls for the conduits. When the concrete was dry, I had to remove the lumber from the wall, which wasn't as easy as it sounds.

Because water in the concrete made the wood swell, it was very difficult to remove the wood. In addition to that, the drawings were wrong and the lumber was inserted in the wrong place in many locations. I had to hand chisel grooves into the concrete by standing on a ladder and chiseling the ceiling above my head all day. That was a lousy job. I had no protection of any kind, so my eyes were full of concrete chips and my arms ached tremendously by the end of the day. We worked 6 days a week.

The last year of high school, I decided to attend a trade school with my friends, Robi Schultz, and Tomi Kemeny to learn filmmaking. I got the equivalent of a B.A. degree in cine-photography. The first job we got was to make a film to recruit people into the Hungarian Air Force.

They took us up in a World War I bi-plane. We took off from the runway, the cold wind swirling against my head and body and the engine roared in my ear. I was hanging out of the seat with a heavy Arriflex camera taped to my body. Back then, those cameras had a lens attached to a box which housed the main components of the camera. Above that was a big figure-eight-shaped compartment that held a full and an empty spool of film that rolled through the box as photos were snapped. It was very bulky compared to the cameras of today. I took pictures of Robi while he did aerobatics in the other plane. My heart was pounding in my chest as we flew. It was such an amazing experience.

As a filmmaker, I also got to go to these amazing, crazy parties with lots of girls who were hired to do acting in the films. They were very fun and always entertaining.

Chapter 5:

Surviving Military Camp

During the school semester we would get a two-hour lecture from the army. They would teach us things like how to assemble and dissemble rifles and handguns with our eyes covered with a band.

In the summer, we would have to spend one month in an army camp.

The army camps were some of the worst conditions I had ever experienced. There were about 3,000 people packed into the camp and since the summer was hot and dry there was never enough water to drink and very little food.

We only had one uniform and since there wasn't any water to bathe, we would have to sleep in our filth every night. We had to get up at 5 am every morning, and because we weren't allowed to keep anything in our tents we had to pack everything up and carry it with us all day.

In addition to that we were made to wear Russian uniforms called 'Zubborkas'. It was a thick, heavy uniform designed for Russia's cold temperatures, not Hungarian summers. We all sweltered in them. We were also given these hard leather army booths but instead of socks we had something called 'kapca' which was no more than a square cloth designed to wrap around the foot and ankle. Unfortunately, nobody knew how to tie them correctly so people kept getting these painful blisters. Thankfully my dad, who had been in the army, taught me to fold the kapca correctly to withstand hours of marching.

We had no toilets, just this one large trench on the outskirts of the camp. It gave off this incredible stink. One soldier, while going to the bathroom, pulled down his pants and as he did so, his wallet slipped out and fell into the trench full of filth. Since it was a crime not to have any identification and it couldn't be replaced, he had no choice but wade through the excrement until he could grab his wallet. And since there was no water to shower, he had to stay in the same clothes for the rest of training.

There were some nurses who worked at the camp. They were the only females around so they got a lot of attention from the soldiers. A group of us decided to play a little trick on them, saying that we had a problem with our butts. The poor nurses had to examine a bunch of naked butts for no reason.

We all spent each day just trying to survive. Life was very cheap in the camps. A mechanical engineer who had a bad heart was made to do all the drills until he died.

During the night, we took turns standing guard. It was a frightening experience because we were right across from the Romanian boarder. The shifts lasted for two hours and we would stay absolutely still, not even daring to breath.

The guards were also in charge of letting the soldiers back in, usually officers who were on leave. There was this one sergeant who none of the soldiers liked. He was abusive and cruel to his underlings. One night he came home drunk and he had forgotten the password to get back into base so the guard on duty shot him dead.

Thankfully I survived the experience and after my time in the army was done, I went to the Technical University of Budapes (Muegyetem) where I studied Mechanical Engineering. University was a fun and amazing experience. I was always good at school so I never had to take it too seriously which meant there was a lot of time for parties and hanging out with girlfriends.

One winter evening, my friends Peter, Robi, Tomi, and I were climbing up a hill to a shelter to spend the night. It was getting dark and cold and we were getting tired. Part way up the hill we heard faint cries for help from the other side of a ravine. We followed the sounds all the way down and up on the other side of the ravine to find them.

What we found was our professor, head of the math department, his wife and two of their small daughters exhausted and lost. We quickly sprang into action. Tomi lifted one girl on his neck, and I pulled the math professor's wife up. Robi ran to get help, while Ivan helped the other daughter. We had to go down the hill again and up on the right side of the ravine. Many skiers came down from the shelter to help us.

The math professor was of course very grateful and offered teaching jobs to Tomi Kemeny and I. We taught mathematics for the rest of our studies there – all seven semesters. I gave lectures on mechanics and physics. I also taught the classes given to laborers in the afternoon, but they were tired after working in a factory all day and disinterested in the subject. I did not like teaching them but I tried my best to make it interesting for them. If they feel asleep, I just left them alone.

To earn more money in the third and fourth years of my studies, I also worked evenings as a draftsman at a heavy railroad car factory, MAVAG. They made locomotives and railroad cars there, all of which were taken to Russia for war retribution.

I still had enough strength to frequently go dancing into the wee hours of the night before going the steam bath at the Gellert hotel, where I had a locker and could sleep until I went to my classes the next day. This steam bath was built by the Romans over 2,000 years ago and is still there in good condition, even today.

I met a wonderful, gorgeous young lady at a dance whose name was Erzsi which in Hungarian is short for Elizabeth. We fell in love and dated for several years. She lived with her mother, who disapproved of us being together, so when we were at Erzsi' house we usually locked the bedroom door so we would not be disturbed. Erzsi was a wonderful and beautiful girl.

During my first year at the Technical University of Budapest, I organized a large party, which was held at the entrance hall of the Gellert Hotel. More than 3,000 people attended, because I advertised that a band would play American jazz music, which was forbidden under communist rule. The hotel staff was worried that we had too many people and the building would not hold them all, but it did fine and we had a good party.

The Gellert has a large staircase in the entrance hall from the gallery. To open the ball, I descended those stairs with Erzsi in a special tuxedo made for the occasion. She was dressed in a beautiful gown and held onto my arm as we strolled down that large staircase. We were received with great applause, which made us feel very special.

That year Erzsi got really bad headaches. Her doctor suspected a brain tumor, but medical care wasn't very reliable back then so I asked around and found a friend who was medical student who said Erzsi was likely misdiagnosed. Her headaches got worse and worse so I checked her into a hospital. The resident brain surgeon of the hospital also expressed his doubts about the diagnoses. He said it wasn't a brain tumor and that the headaches would go away naturally which they did.

Erzsi wanted to get married and have a family but I wasn't ready. I thought I was too young. After she became healthy and I left Hungary, the brain surgeon married Erzsi and they had two children together. She named the first one Tomi. When I heard about that it made me very happy, because that is what she used to call me.

Next, I was introduced by a friend to Judy. Like many university students everywhere, we explored our sexuality. Judy and I celebrated her 16th birthday with great sex. We heard the door open and footsteps. Her parents had come home unexpectedly. I had to collect my clothes and jump out the window onto the ledge. I hastily put my clothes back on and ran home.

We continued our clandestine relationship. Judy got pregnant and since abortions were illegal at that time, I had her sit behind me on my motorcycle and we drove through some very bumpy cobblestone roads. It felt like the drive lasted forever. I had many different thoughts going through my mind. I'm sure Judy did as well. Afterward the procedure was completed, we were very relieved. This unwanted outcome was what my father danced around about when he yelled at me in the square so many years ago. I'm thankful my father never found out about this. He would have been disappointed for sure.

Chapter 6:

My Photography Years

After graduating from the Technical University of Budapest with a degree in Mechanical Engineering in 1955, the state wanted to send me to a small power station somewhere in the mountains. I received state grants for 3-1/2 years of my education, so I was obligated to take the job they provided. However, I did not want to leave Budapest, so I went underground and became a photographer.

I formed a partnership with two other guys. One was the salesman who traveled the country visiting nurseries full of young children. He charmed the nurses and would set up a day for me to go in and take pictures of all the kids. The nurses would tell the kids to let their parents know that a photographer was coming on a certain day and they should dress nicely. I would ride my motorcycle to the location and take pictures. Some kids were dressed in every day clothes while others were specially dressed up for the occasion. I took pictures of all of them regardless of what they wore.

I very carefully took a picture of each child so as not to frighten him or her. If one child started to cry, they all cried and my trip was wasted. I photographed everyone, including the nurses. I was always hopeful that the nurses would express their gratitude by spending time with me in the evening.

When I got back to Budapest, the third guy developed and printed the pictures overnight and made up three postcards of each person. The next morning, we sold the three postcards to the sales guy for eight forints each, the Hungarian currency. One of my business associates then went back to the nursery and sold as many pictures as he could for twenty forints a set. Sometimes he made money, sometimes not. Either way, we all had a lot of fun.

During this time, I would walk the boulevards in the evening with two cameras on my shoulder offering to take free pictures of all the pretty women telling them they could apply to become models or actresses if they had a good picture. None of the ladies ever refused, as far as I can recall, although some husbands gave me nasty looks.

I asked this one woman if I could take her picture and she took me back to her apartment where I photographed her. She then took off all her clothes and I snapped several pictures of her naked. She was extremely attractive and seductive. Afterwards we started to kiss. Soon we were in bed together. We then heard the creak of the door open. It was her husband returning home from work. I quickly grabbed my clothes and jumped out the window.

*　　　*　　　*　　　*

My father kept pestering me to continue my engineering career and that my photography wasn't sustainable, but I still didn't want to leave Budapest. Eventually, I relented, realizing that he was right. I needed to make more money and I didn't want to be a photographer.

I was offered a job by the government as a Shift Charge Engineer at the new power station of Stalintown, south of Budapest on the bank of the Danube. The Chief Engineer was in political jail, so I ended up in charge of the power station as the acting Chief Engineer. I never learned what happened to the Chief Engineer or why he had been imprisoned.

At a typical power plant, there was a Chief Engineer and four Shift Charge Engineers. We had to work 7 days from 6am to 2pm then we got one-and-a-half days off. Next, we had 5-night shifts with

24 hours off. Then we rotated to 6-afternoon shifts before starting the cycle all over again.

At 24 years old, I was the oldest Shift Charge engineer so when the Chief Engineer was arrested I was put in charge of the entire power plant. I wasn't very prepared for handling the problems that I encountered on my very first day.

This newly built city, Stalintown, was located about 20 miles south of Budapest on the west bank of the Danube River. The industrial complex included Bessemer furnaces to produce steel. These large furnaces removed impurities from molten pig iron by blowing air into the hot iron, producing steel. The power station had coal-fire furnaces designed to be fed pulverized coal, but were started to be lit with oil burners.

The coal was imported from Russia and was of very poor quality. A lot of the coal was mixed with mud. The lousy coal frequently broke the mills that were used to grind it into powder. In addition, the heat energy contained in the muddy coal was low, so the oil burners were often used to keep the fire alive. The Russian coal was piled up outdoors and fed onto a conveyor belt using an overhead bridge crane, which was delivered to the furnaces. The bridge cranes were operated by women who sat in their cubicles about 80 feet above the ground for an 8-hour shift. The women did this job during the winter in freezing weather with no heat in their cubicle. It was terrible working conditions, but it was a job when work was scarce so most did it without complaints.

The station had five 20-Megawatt steam turbines, about five stories high, each produced electrical power. The power station was designed for these generators, but only two were in service. Another generator was delivered shortly after my arrival there. After the installation of it was completed, I had to synchronize it with the two generators already in operation, which made up the grid.

I coupled it up to the grid by watching the rotational speed of the turbine in a display. When that turbine reached exactly 3,000 revolutions per minute and got in phase with the grid, I had to manually turn the generator on the grid. This was a very difficult process and it was the first time I had tried this. I was very apprehensive and wasn't sure I could do it, but unfortunately, there was nobody else trained. I maneuvered everything into place. The turbine reached 3,000 revolutions per minute and I flipped the switch to turn the third generator on.

But things didn't go as planned and the turbine exploded. There was a big cloud of smoke and a fire, rocking the whole station. Parts of the generator went through the roof. I was stunned and shocked. I rushed towards the turbine to look at the damage. The explosion killed the shop foreman and several workers.

I felt very guilty until after I learned that the turbine was made in Czechoslovakia for Austria, but was rejected because of poor quality, so Hungary bought it at a discount. An investigation revealed that the valve regulating the amount of steam entering the turbine failed and stuck in the open position. The excess steam over sped the turbine beyond the desired 3,600 rpm, until the centrifugal force tore the rotor apart. It disintegrated at high speed, sending the metal bits into the room like shrapnel. I was vindicated, but the country was still short on electrical power.

This was the first major accident during my work there, but not the last. We had an accident about once a week and once a month somebody was sure to be killed or maimed. For example, the cleaning woman sweeping around the switchgear, which were charged with 50,000 volts, saw a dead mouse under a disconnect switch. She reached in with the handle bar of her broom and was burned to charcoal.

My friend, Peter, who had graduated as a civil engineer by this time, was also stationed there for two years. He left soon after I got there, so we had a farewell dinner for him at the best bar in the area. We ate steak, which was quite expensive at that time.

As we ate, a drunken guy entered the bar and attempted to 'cut in' on a couple that was dancing, despite a sign on the wall that very clearly said 'NO CUTTING IN!' Immediately a fight began which everyone in the room joined – fighting was one of the best types of entertainment back then. Peter decided we should not give up our expensive steaks, so he and I tipped our table on its side, sat on the floor in a corner behind the table and finished eating our dinner. Eventually, the police showed up and arrested the guy who tried to cut in. Two hours later, he was back, drunk as a skunk, worse than before. That is when Peter and I decided it was time for us to leave.

Around that time, I shared an apartment with another engineer. We liked to solve problems by 'engineering' creative solutions. Since our apartment had no hot water, we decided to throw a steel hook over the high-tension power line outside of our window, then ran a cable from the hook to the water in our bathtub and let the current in that cable heat the water in the tub. Looking back on it, it sounds crazy but we took hot baths and no one was electrocuted.

In 1955, there was a significant earthquake, causing major damage, which toppled every chimney in Hungary. I was in my bed sleeping at the time and I was thrown to the floor. I thought another turbine blew up at the power station, so I got up and scrambled into the station to help. It turned out the Bessemer tower, the huge steel furnace about 6 stories high, used to melt pig iron, broke during the earthquake and all the liquid iron poured out onto the ground. A locomotive near the Bessemer was melted to the rails of the train track. It took months to fix everything.

When I became a Shift Charge Engineer at the power station in Stalintown, I drove my Rommel Zundapp motorcycle home every time I had a few days off. General Rommel, the popular German field marshal of World War II, had the German motorcycle factory Zundapp produce special units for the desert war in Africa. After the war, some of the damaged "Rommel Zundapp" motorcycles were abandoned by the Germans. I found one with a functional engine and a broken gearbox. There were no parts available, so I fashioned a gear from a round piece of steel by hand using a file. It was very crude, but it worked for a while.

I would drive to Budapest and spend time with my girlfriend. One time I was having a conversation while holding the bike and it fell over, pinning my hand under the handbrake on the handlebar. My right hand was punctured next to my thumb. I had to walk to the hospital where I was given a tetanus shot in my left shoulder. The shot hurt more than the punctured hand so I went around with my left arm in a sling. I had fun answering people when they asked what happened to me. I would say that I punctured my right hand. They would usually ask why my left arm was in a sling when it was my right hand that got hurt. My answer was 'they are trying to fix the hand, which hurts more.'

Another weekend while driving to Budapest at about 20 kilometers per hour, one of my testicles started to really hurt when I arrived at my destination. All medical services in Hungary were free, so I went to a hospital for help. The doctor diagnosed me with testicular cancer and suggested I have it removed immediately to avoid cancer from spreading to the other testicle. This obviously left me very distressed. Since I did not trust the free medical system, I consulted a doctor friend of mine. He said I was sitting on the motorcycle saddle too long and should sit in a tub of cold water for a while. Fortunately, my doctor friend was right. He saved me one testicle which I'm very grateful for!

Chapter 7:

Pursuing My Dream To Be An Engineer

There simply was not enough power most of the time, so Hungary imported power from Czechoslovakia, Austria, and Russia. But even with the power from those countries, we had constant blackouts. The grid was often overloaded and the system frequency, which was normally 50 hertz, would slow down.

The total power generated by all stations was about 900 megawatts. To put that into perspective, one generator at the Redondo Beach California station generates about 2,000 MW alone. At its worst, the frequency would lag and fall below 50 hertz. We could not avoid a full blackout. If we lost power from Czechoslovakia, our main supplier, we would reduce the load by cutting off some customers (what we call brown-outs here in the States). The junior engineer was responsible for cutting off power to citizens. It would often be a very difficult responsibility deciding who got power and who didn't.

When we took too much power from Czechoslovakia, we would get angry calls from their Central Control saying that if we did not reduce the load they would cut Hungary off completely. When that happened, we had a prioritized list of customers to cut off first, second, and so on. The last on the list were hospitals and the military. Turning off power was a very frequent occurrence, but we managed.

Around this time, I got tired of my Zundapp and finally got a real motorcycle, a 500 cc BMW, which was a big upgrade. It would do 50 mph on a good day and I learned to race it on a dirt track. My instructor chased me around and knocked the rear wheel out from under me when I did not go fast enough.

I added a sidecar to the BMW and raced it on a dirt track with a "mitfahrer" — 'fellow rider' in German — sitting on a sidecar frame and leaning as far as he could to balance the rig. Then I had a great idea, Motorcycles without sidecars could lean into the corners, but sidecars prevented leaning, So I attached my sidecar to the bike with pivot joints and added a steering wheel to the sidecar so the "mitfahrer" could control the lean. It worked for a few rounds, but the pivot joints were not strong enough and the sidecar got detached going through a sharp curve. I went left on the motorcycle while a guy we called Kocka, (the Cube in English, because he was large and heavy like a cube,) who was my "mitfahrer" went right—and straight through the wood fence. Thankfully, he was uninjured.

In 1956, I had the first vacation from my job as Shift Charge Engineer at the Central Power Station of Stalintown and went to visit Czechoslovakia. I particularly wanted to visit the Tatra Mountains in Slovakia. Before I got the BMW motorcycle, I had my very small NSU motorcycle and no money.

Quality wrist watches were scarce in Czechoslovakia, so I bought about 20 watches on the black market in Budapest which I planned to sell once I reached my destination. They were mostly premium Swiss-made Doxa watches, which I hid in the motorcycle. If they were noticed, I could be arrested, so I disassembled the motorcycle's battery by carefully taking the grids out. The grids consisted of lead plates that create electricity by reacting with an acid mixture. I packed the watches at the bottom of the battery case, sealed the bottom part, cut the lead plates to fit the now smaller case and re-installed them. The battery worked but had less capacity due to its smaller size.

With enough money in my pocket to buy gasoline but not much more, I slowly drove north. At full throttle, the bike could do only about 15 miles per hour. I was supposed to meet a friend and his wife at the top of the Tatra Mountains. These are the highest mountains in Poland, and are part of Carpathian Mountains that create a natural border between Slovakia and Poland.

The border guards became very suspicious because I did not exchange Hungarian currency to Czech money. They asked me how I was going to live, and I told them I had some friends who would feed and help me. The guards did not believe me, so they completely disassembled my bike looking for contraband. I was extremely nervous as they checked the lights, took the tires off and even took the gas tank off and emptied it. When they finally let me go, I had to re-assemble the bike along the roadside. Thankfully I always carried tools and was able to salvage and use the gasoline.

I met my friends at our rendezvous in the mountains, but unfortunately, nobody was interested in buying the watches I had so carefully carried with me. I borrowed enough money for a plane ticket to Prague and flew in a very small propeller plane, which could barely handle the 6,000ft altitude. I arrived in Prague, not knowing anyone and with no money. Nobody could speak Hungarian or German, so I mainly used sign language. Eventually, I found the main square where people were selling black market items. I sold all the watches, as best I could, and after looking around for a day, flew back to Slovakia to the Tatra Mountains to meet my friends again.

We heard that there was an observatory on the top of the tallest peak and anyone could pay to ride a cable car up to there, so we decided to try it. First, a cable car for about 20 passengers took us to the bottom of the peak. We then got on another cable car that took only four people at a time up to the top. This cable car, or gondola, was a little box maybe eight feet by eight feet. When they started to pack several days of food, water, and other supplies into the gondola, we thought it was for the observatory. They explained that supplies for the observatory were hoisted on another cable. The food and water they were loading were for us in case we got stranded partway up. Not very reassuring.

If there was high wind, the car had to be stopped. It ran on a very old, single loop cable about 2,500 feet long and was stabilized by another cable so if the wind velocity was over a mere five miles-an-hour, the cable and the gondola would swing and become unstable. The delay was totally weather dependent. A guard was always on board, so the three of us filled up the 4-person cabin. They had us sign a release confirming that they were not responsible for anything that might happen.

On a normal swing, you feel the forward and backward, or side to side motion, but in the cable car, you didn't feel any movement. You can't see the movement of the car either. What happens is that you look outside and see the whole mountain going sideways - you are the center of the world and the mountain is moving relative to you. It was a very strange feeling. After a while, the wind started to swing the gondola. Now the rock wall was moving down and left, then down and right and back again. When the wind increased beyond the critical value of 5 mph, the rock wall stopped moving down; it just swung from left to right and back. Of course, we were stopped.

Several hours after we got out of the gondola, the wind had died down and we continued up to towards the peak. The observatory was on the largest peak and it was a long hike. But it was well worth it. The view was extraordinarily beautiful. We were standing on this mountain and everywhere you looked was down, several thousand feet down. Thankfully it was an extremely clear day. There were several peaks with little bridges between them. We had to walk on those little bridges from peak to peak. Each bridge was smaller than a small room and you had to use them to get to the next peak where there might be a cafeteria to get something to eat. We would look down and see the people in a valley below harvesting. They looked very tiny way down there.

As an engineer, I wondered how the bridges were built. There were incredible structured, much better than what was being built under the communist regime. We followed the pathway until we got to the observatory. The observatory had a reasonable-sized telescope. The primary mirror was maybe 36 inches. The telescope was constructed many years before and I asked the soldiers how they got it up there. They told me it had to be carried up, piece by piece, and assembled on the top of the mountain.

Down at the bottom of the valley were green pastures and villages. The air was so clear we had the impression we could just reach down and touch the roofs of the houses. It felt like you could step down into that world. It was like the villages were part of a small train set. You could see everything, but there was no sound.

The gondola ride back down was uneventful. Thankfully we didn't get stuck in the gondola. The trip home was long and boring on the slow motorcycle.

Chapter 8:

Hungarian Revolution

I arrived home from Czechoslovakia on a Tuesday to learn that the university students wanted to demonstrate in favor of Polish Freedom Fighters. The political leader of Hungary, Mátyás Rakosi, was in Moscow at the time. The person in charge denied permission to the demonstrators to leave the grounds of the Technical University, but as the crowd grew bigger and bigger, he changed his mind. The procession of demonstrators walked from the University in Buda across the bridge and marched on what is called the Inner Circle Boulevard (Kis Korut) towards the square where a Polish general's statue stood.

By the time the student protesters reached the statue it was afternoon and many workers joined the parade after their morning shift, which ended at 2 p.m. The streets became packed with people, shoulder to shoulder. There was a lot of energy in the air. People were chanting and marching, waving signs in the air. Some held the portrait of Imre Nagy, a reformist, who a lot of the students and workers urged to take charge. Hungarian flags with the communist emblem torn out were waved overhead.

Once again, the person in charge changed his mind and sent police to stop the demonstration. When that failed, he ordered the army to help the police because they had nine old T-34 Russian tanks left over from the Second World War. I arrived just when the tanks met the crowd, head on, at the Inner Circle Boulevard near our home.

I recognized two of the tank drivers from when I was a Second Lieutenant for the armored division. They were about two years younger and I had trained them as tank drivers during my military summer camp. I walked up to them with my hands in the air. I felt that they could see me through the opening on the driver's side of the tank.

I yelled 'Hey guys, what are you doing?'

I knew they would stop if they recognized me, and they did. Soon the tank officers understood what was happening and joined the demonstration rather than stopping it with the tanks.

These events can be seen in the movie "Sunshine", a story about three generations of a Jewish-Hungarian family. It is a combination of acted scenes interwoven with documentary footage taken at this event. In the movie, an actor is shown walking up to the tanks and stopping them.

That evening a few of the revolutionary leaders emerged and decided to march to the studios of the state radio station. They wanted to announce to the country that a revolution was taking place in Budapest. The delegation approached the building, under a white flag, to request permission to make the announcement. Snipers from the roof of the studio building open fired, killing the delegation. This was the beginning of the fighting.

In the first round of fighting, the communists were quickly defeated. Pro-soviet communists were either executed or imprisoned. Russian troops, which were stationed in Hungary since the end of WWII, mostly outside of Budapest, had learned Hungarian by that time and had many friends in the country. The Russian soldiers were sympathetic to the motivation behind the revolution and did not join the fight.

Fighting started on October 23 and ended November 10. Afterwards, there was relative calm which lasted for several weeks. During that time, everybody was happy. Many businesses had broken windows from the fighting, but nobody looted. In fact, people sometimes threw money through the broken windows to help the small businesses with repairs.

At that time, my father had been promoted to the position of Chief Auditor for the Ministry of Agriculture. As matters gradually returned to normal, he also went back to work. I was a Junior Engineer at the state-owned Consulting Engineering firm which was in charge of designing and running all of the central power generating stations for Hungary.

After the two-year engagement as Shift Change Engineer was completed, I quit and went back to Budapest, where Dr. Heller, my former professor at the university, was the Director of Central Power Generation and Control for Hungary. He hired me to control the electric power distribution for the entire country. It was a prestigious job that even provided me with permission to own a car and purchase gasoline.

My office was close to the Ministry of Agriculture, which was on a large square at the center of Pest. Sometimes I walked over and had lunch with my father at the Ministry. As matters became calm, I called my father one day in October 1956 and arranged to meet him.

At the same time, two different army groups arrived at the square where the Ministry was located. Both the Hungarian and the Russian armies wore the same uniform so it was difficult to tell which army was shooting at whom. Unfortunately, a major misunderstanding developed and the two groups started to shoot at each other with machine guns, cannons, and tank fire.

There were many people in the square going about their business at lunchtime who got caught in the crossfire. I was close to the main gate of the Ministry of Agriculture, so I tried to get in. However, the people inside the Ministry had closed the gate to avoid being shot. I almost panicked but kept my wits about me. I noticed a cannon on a tank at the other side of the square that was aimed at the Ministry and was systematically shooting at the crowds. I anticipated that the next shot could be aimed at about where I was standing, next to the wall of the Ministry. In desperation, I climbed over several dead bodies up to the level of the windows and dived in, head first, smashing through the closed double pane windows. The shots flew past me, hitting exactly where I had been standing seconds before.

I gathered myself and ran to open the gate to let people in. A crowd rushed through the gate, but the next shot from the cannon came right through the gate and killed them all.

I went to look for my father, who I learned later had left the Ministry through a back door and was already headed home. No doubt he was expecting that I had gone home, too. When I did eventually get home and my parents saw me covered with blood from the cuts on my head and hands, they put me to bed. I stayed in bed for several days. There was very little I could remember. I must have had a concussion, but could not let that stop me. When I finally became aware of my surroundings, I realized that most of my hair had fallen out.

Many people died unnecessarily in the square. One of my friends, my childhood tutor, Vamos Bandy, was shot in the stomach and lay in the square for hours. Fortunately, he survived.

Someone asked me when I made the conscious decision to live my life to the best of my ability and just make every moment count. I think this experience was probably it. How often do you climb over dead bodies to save your own life and then try to help others only to see them die, too?

During the next few weeks, life returned to normal and my hair grew back. People went to work, to shop and went about their business. Newspapers started back up, political parties were formed and everybody ignored the inevitable future – the Soviet Union gearing up for an attack. Despite the raw emotions and all the destruction, there was no crime in the city. People continued to throw money into the broken store windows to help business owners pay for the damage caused by the revolution. There was no political process at all. We knew we had to form a government before the Soviet Union attacked us so trusted people were called to take charge. The former Minister of Agriculture, Imre Nagy, was persuaded to become the Prime Minister.

At the same time, there were rumors the Russians were modifying the railroad rails from the Ukrainian border towards Budapest. The Russian railroad had wider tracks than the rest of the world, so at the Hungarian/Ukrainian border locomotives and the undercarriage of the cars was always changed. Nobody paid attention. We were simply happy to have our freedom.

When England attacked at the Suez Canal, the world's attention was diverted from Hungary. The next day, fresh Soviet troops entered Hungary. These troops, with no ties to Hungarians, were reserves called in for the occasion. They were told that Hungarians were attacked by rotten capitalists and their job was to free us. None of these troops spoke Hungarian and were poorly trained and poorly equipped. Their communication gear was particularly bad. They frequently lost contact with their superiors and comrades.

As the fresh troops approached Budapest, we could hear cannons in the distance, gradually coming closer. Some Hungarians appealed to the USA, but most of us believed the USA was not going to start a third world war over Hungary.

The Hungarian army had 9 worn-out WWII Soviet T-34 tanks for training purposes. Those nine T-34s were left behind in Hungary by the Soviets came in handy. Since I was familiar with driving then, I ended up aligning one tank after the other at the foot of Gellert Mountain facing the incoming Russian tanks. In retrospect, some of those tanks were probably the same I had stopped by waving my hands at the drivers. By now it was November and the concussion I suffered after jumping through the window of the Ministry in October had healed.

These T34 tanks did not have steering wheels. Instead, they had two levers, one on each side of the driver to control the tank with. Shoving one forward and pulling one back spun the tank on its tracks. These levers had long rods at the floor coupling them to the drives and brakes. The driver's foot rested between these rods.

There was a small rectangular hole in front of the driver protected by thick armor. To get in or out the tank, the driver had to lower his body through this hole lifting himself and twisting his body as he got through the small opening. I was quite excited to be in one of these again and as I was getting out, my right foot got stuck between the steering rods. I twisted my right knee and tore it. My knee swelled up like a melon. I was limited in what I could do after that, so I put my girlfriend on the back of my motorcycle with a camera and we drove around taking pictures of the fighting.

I had other girlfriends in that period. Once I had an experienced partner who taught me a lot, particularly about paying attention to my partner's needs to assure that I satisfy her. That was very good advice. I had a good friend who had a very pretty girlfriend that he did not properly satisfy. She was very miserable so I slept with her and she was very satisfied. Times were very hard and every moment mattered. We did what we could to enjoy ourselves.

The Russians came in from the east, entering Budapest with tanks and armored vehicles we called 'duck-chasers'. The duck-chasers were trucks armored on the front and side but had only canvas tops. Hungarians dropped hand grenades from the upper floors of apartment houses onto the trucks, frequently breaking the canvas top and killing the soldiers inside. The armored tanks were more difficult to disable. We were familiar with T-34s. They were poorly designed and built quickly, likely because Stalin's strategy was to have a huge quantity of tanks, even if that meant his army had tanks of less quality than the German 'Tigers'. Stalin disagreed with Hitler's philosophy that to win the war the army had to have the *largest and best* tanks. There is no question now which of them had the right strategy.

The T-34 turrets were only held to the chassis by three clips. There was a gap between the bottom at the back of the turret and the top of the chassis. Even a hand-grenade exploded in this gap toppled the turret off the chassis, disabling the tank. Also, the canon was very long. Brave Hungarians approached the tanks from the blind spots and hung their bodyweight on the end of the cannon using a rag to prevent burning their hands. Two guys could unbalance and topple a turret by swinging on the canon. They could then kill the exposed soldiers inside. There were usually three people inside: the driver; the officer, who sat above the driver in the turret, who steered the driver with his feet on the driver's shoulders; and the ammunition handler, who sat to next to the officer. Another weak spot of the T-

34 was its blind spot in the back. Anybody brave enough could run up from the back, step up on the rear deck using the rear protrusions, and place a hand-grenade into the gap under the turret.

Most of the Russian tanks invading Hungary were newer T-52 tanks. They were much better than the T-34s, and we were not familiar with them. The only effective way to stop them was to blow off the treads they were running on. Hungarian kids used their mother's frying pans to do that. By turning the pans upside-down and placing them in the middle of the road with a string attached, they would hide on both sides of the road in coal cellars, pulling the strings to move the frying pans in the way of the tank. The view from the tank was poor and the pans looked like they could have been landmines. The tanks tried to avoid the pans, but the kids would move the pans in line with the tank's treads. Sometimes the tank just gave up and backed away.

During the fighting, enough Russian soldiers were killed to cover the road about 2 feet high. Wave after wave of tanks just continued coming and driving over the dead bodies until the Hungarian revolution was quelled.

At the height of the revolution, there were about 2,000 Russian tanks in Budapest. To put that number into context, Hitler had fewer tanks during the German invasion of Russia from the Black Sea to the North Sea. There was a tank virtually at every street corner.

The Russian reservists were young and jumpy. They would open fire at the slightest noise. This was extremely dangerous for anybody caught in the line of fire, often hitting civilians unlucky enough to be in the wrong place at the wrong time. One time, a lineup of women waiting to buy food were gunned down. The situation was chaotic and was getting more dangerous as the days progressed, especially for young men known to oppose Communism.

Chapter 9:

Escaping Communism

After the Soviet invasion had swept through the country, life became very miserable in Hungary. Thousands were imprisoned, some were sent to Russian gulags, and the worst offenders were executed. Those who could leave Hungary fled the country after the Revolution in 1956. Some 200,000 people escaped, mostly educated professionals. Most of them wanted to immigrate to the US through Austria, although some escaped towards Yugoslavia too.

Those who didn't have enough money or educated enough were left behind. Many peopled died unnecessarily, trying to escape communism. One of my girlfriends left with another friend on a motorcycle and tried to make a run through the border. We were told they were mercilessly machine-gunned to death. A swimming champion tried to jump overboard a ship on the Danube and swim for it. He couldn't make it and drowned.

I was always very social and had many friends. Our group of friends would watch each other, silently wondering who was going to leave next. My accident from the tank was still delaying me so I was forced to watch as one by one, my friends left the country until only my best friend, Peter Grosz, and I seemed to be the only ones left in Budapest. We kept calling each other waiting to see who was going to make a run for it first.

One day my father told me he had called Peter who had said cryptically he was leaving the country with his wife, who he had just recently married. Next day I left, alone, heading for the Austrian border. I told nobody except my parents. They were sad to see me go but they understood my reasoning for getting out of the country. There was no future for me in Hungary. I got on a train going west towards the Austrian border at Hegyeshalom.

On the train, I met another one of my friends, Vamos Bandi who really did not want to leave the country, but his wife was already in Vienna. He had heard that she was being held for ransom and her parents would have to pay. There were many thieves at the time praying on people's misfortunes.

I had a compass and a map – both considered military secrets, stolen from the army – and a small necklace, the last jewelry my mother had given to me to help me survive. I heard a lot of stories of émigrés paying the local farmers at the border to help them across, only to have them misled and abandoned them. We decided we would find our way on our own with the help of the map and compass. On the train, three other young men joined us.

There were three border patrols as we approached the Austrian border. The first one was at about 10 kilometers from the border and it consisted of a checkpoint on the roads and railroads. The second one, at about five kilometers from the border, consisted of walking patrols. Lastly, at the border, there was a wide bare strip with barbed wire, lookout posts on tall wooden towers with heavy machine guns. The patrols would stay hidden for a time then moved to a different spot on a pre-arranged schedule.

When we got within 10 kilometers of the border, we were getting concerned about the checkpoints. We decided to hide between two rail cars hanging on the air hoses connecting the cars. When we arrived at the checkpoint, we could see the soldiers walking up and down on the platform and questioning the passengers in the cars, asking for proof of either living near the border or permits to enter that border zone. I held my breath that we were not discovered.

At the next stop, we got off the train and hide in the bushes until it got dark. It was raining which was both a blessing and a curse as it hid us from any board guards, but it made waiting long and damp.

We began walking towards the border using my compass and map as a guide. It was an especially dark, moonless night and so we were able to move in relative obscurity. Eventually, we saw Russian soldiers sitting at campfires in the distance and occasionally shooting flares up. We guessed we were at the border. We laid down in the mud and started to crawl like we were taught in the army. We tried to avoid the campfires and every time a flare went up we laid still.

After several kilometers, we got close to a village. We were very concerned that accidentally we crawled back to Hungary, so we cautiously looked at the street signs. When we saw the street signs in German, we realized we were in Austria. We had done it.

It was early morning and it was beginning to get light. We walked around the village looking for some sign of life. We found one bar still open with people drinking. We went in and were recognized as refugees from the mud and dirt and our language. I was the only who could speak some German. We were hoping somebody would buy us some food, but they only offered us drinks.

One man befriended us and eventually offered us shelter in his home. His wife was on a trip, so he was alone. It turned out he was a Nazi and he was very proud of it. He showed us the gun he had hidden away, in case the Russian try to come back again. Luckily, he did not recognize me as a Jew; he was very much an anti-Semite and associated the communists with the Jews. We went to sleep finally next morning, but never got any food.

Next morning my companions became worried about not having legal papers. I kept saying we didn't need any papers, nobody will ask for papers in a free country, but they insisted we check into some organization. We found that the refugees were directed to the local school, where they were processed and recorded. We went there and soon found ourselves in what seemed like a concentration camp. They fed us a little bit, but there were no showers and it was impossible to find out what would happen to us.

After five days, I decided they could stay, but I was going. I was worried that the US special quota for refugees will be closed soon and I wanted to get to Vienna where the US Embassy was located. Three of the guys stayed at the camp. I do not know what happened to them. My friend wanted to find his wife in Vienna, so the two of us escaped by climbing under the barbed wire where the sewer from the toilets existed. We flagged down a pickup truck on the highway and got a ride to Vienna.

Vienna was overloaded with refugees. The US Embassy did not let anybody enter; all you could do was register. The two of us slept on benches, mostly in the Westbahnhof (railroad station) when the policeman allowed us in. We slept one night at some preacher's home, who fed us dinner. One day I had half a sandwich from a young child on a street car. I could not help staring at her eating, so she offered me her sandwich. Refugees traveled free on public transportation. I also got some chestnuts from an old lady selling roasted chestnuts on a street corner. It tasted delicious.

I sold my mother's necklace and we bought a pistol to help us persuade my friend's wife's captors to give her up. I don't know the full details of the story, but my friend, Vamos Bandi, found his wife, helped her escape somehow and returned to Hungary with her. I lost contact with them and don't know what happened to them afterwards.

Chapter 10:

My Life In London

I went to the English Embassy to find out if I could immigrate to Great Britain. To my surprise, I found my old high school teacher translating for the refugees. She asked me to help translate since I could speak some English. I spent considerable effort trying to find my friend Peter Grosz, who I heard was also in Vienna, but I could never track him down.

On the ninth day, I was told the US quota was full and will only be extended when the US legislation decided. My former high school teacher told me the last refugee flight to England was departing soon and she reserved a seat if I wanted. After much deliberation and consideration, I decided to go. I already had a friend in London who I could look up.

We took a flight on the new Constellation airplane to England. They fed us very well. When we arrived, we were taken to another refugee camp; however, we could come and go as we pleased. I decided I had enough of refugee camps and left immediately and got a ride to London. I went directly to the University of London, hoping to find my friend, Peter Wonke.

As I was standing in line, a gentleman noticed that I was talking in English and overheard that I was from Hungary. He approached me and told me his wife asked him to find a refugee baby they could take care of. I told him that it would be very unlikely to find an orphan baby away from their mother

He thought that was a good point and asked me if I would have dinner with them that night. Maybe his wife would be satisfied helping me instead of a baby.

I went with him and found that he was a Greek-born banker living in a large "flat" in Regent Square, in relative luxury, with servants.

I took a bath, which was great since I was filthy after nine days of living in camps and on the streets. To my surprise, the bathroom window could not be closed. It was very cold outside so I asked the butler to help me, but was told the window had not been closed for many years and was painted in the open position. Anyhow, they could not understand why I would close the window because I couldn't get fresh air. I took the bath and got a terrible cold that lasted for days. But at least I was clean.

I was given an old suit since my clothes were tattered. They also helped me to get a job at Babcock and Wilcox as a test engineer and I was assigned to work at the Battersea Power Station to test commercial furnaces. They also helped me to open a bank account at the Barkley's Bank and deposited 30 pounds in my name.

I stayed with them for a few weeks. They had a very old parrot, which could fluently swear in several languages. During a dinner party I attended there, every time a guest set down on a chair the parrot made the squeaky sound of the chair *before* the guest sat down, to the amusement of everybody.

I also managed to amuse the guests by calling the fruit that was being served "ananas" (bananas), which was the name we used in Hungary. I did not realize the potential meaning of that word in English.

They had a son about 17 years old who showed me around London. Once he took me to Soho. As we were looking into a shop window, three drunken sailors attacked us. One of them broke my nose. (Not a big deal since it was broken in fights before), but I was worried about getting into a fight because I did not have permanent residency papers. The "bobbies" showed up very fast and hauled everybody to court to sort things out. It was all very efficient. No arrest, not solicitors, no delay. The court was open in Soho all night; they had plenty of problems to take care of.

I was very concerned the judge will throw me out of the country. He listened to everybody and then sent a court clerk to get the sailor's officer. When the officer arrived, at about 2 am, the judge released the sailors to his custody and we were all told to go home. Thankfully there weren't any consequences.

After several weeks, I found some of my very good friends Frici and Erica Lorant (who were married), Peter Kolbusz and Peter Wonke with his girlfriend Kati. We all got together and rented a flat in Maida Vail. We all had work and managed to enjoy ourselves.

I saved some money and with a loan from Barkley's bought a small motorcycle. It was a great little motorcycle. I rode it everywhere, rain or shine.

Kati and Peter Wonke were architects. They broke up and Peter left for Holland, where his mother lived. Afterwards, I dated Kati for a short while.

I was invited to parties and was a big hit with the women, especially with the ones who liked to talk a lot. My English was only good enough for technical subjects and subjects that I was familiar with. Once a girl changed the subject I was lost, so all I could do to listen. The girls all thought I was sensitive and good at understanding them.

At one of these parties, one of the Hungarian refugees, who I knew, but was not close friends with, took a trip to Paris. When he came home, he told us an unbelievable story.

He had very little money, but the last night in Paris he decided to have a good meal. To his surprise, the waiter told him a beautiful lady at the next table wanted him to join her, which he did. They ended up in her home, where after some drinks she excused herself and came back naked except for a pair of roller skates. She danced around for a while, but finally they got down to business and had a good time. Needless to say, we did not believe him.

*   *   *   *

Eventually, I met a charming young lady and we dated for a while. I was not aware that she was the daughter of the retired Chancellor of Exchequer. They lived in a very good neighborhood and there was always a "bobby" in front of the gate. The bobby only asked my name once and after that he only saluted whenever I arrived. Her mother objected to her riding behind me on the motorcycle, so she ordered their chauffeur to drive us around. She worked in an undergarment factory, which was not a distinguished profession. Once, she also waited for me for two hours in the pouring rain to arrive on my motorcycle when I was late from work.

The final straw with her parents came when they arrived home unexpectedly to find us on the floor in the thralls of passion. I was told to get out.

Eventually, my friends and I decided to give up the apartment. I found a townhouse at 37 Molineux Street, which was rented by five bachelors. Every time one of them got married, they took another bachelor in. After I attended one man's wedding it was my turn to live there.

My twisted right knee was getting worse and worse. I kept falling down the stairs. Medical service was free to everybody in England, but the waiting list was years for anything not life threatening unless you could pay for the treatment.

Since I was a Hungarian refuge I got special attention because many English felt responsible for the Suez Canal Crisis which contributed to the collapse of the Hungarian revolution. I was seen by a doctor immediately. In the hospital, they cut my knee open and removed the broken pieces of cartridges. I was in a ward with thirty-one other patients. During the night, there were only two nurses, including for those who were dying. Since I was relatively well with only my right leg in a cast, I placed my right leg on a dolly and hopped along and helped the nurses during the night.

There were three bedrooms in the house we shared. The oldest tenant had his own bedroom on the third floor. I had my bedroom on the second floor with another guy. On the ground floor was a kitchen and living room.

Every night somebody cooked or his girlfriend cooked for everybody. Saturday afternoon we all went to the nearby pub, played darts and drank room temperature beer. I did not like warm beer but cold beer, lager, was too expensive, so I drank cheap gin. I got really used to the taste, and still drink gin to this day. After the pub, we would go home and cook dinner.

On Sunday, we always selected a party from an array of invitations that we would place on the mantelpiece. The first time it was my turn to cook, I decided to prepare "chicken paprikas" to give them a taste of Hungary. The only problem was I did not know how to cook. In desperation, I called my mother in Hungary. To my great surprise, the call went through and my mother explained what to do. What she did not know was that in my apartment everybody cooked everything with a pressure cooker. Since I didn't know any better I put the chicken and the potatoes into the pressure cooker and put it on the fire.

When it was cooking, I found that I could not open the pot. I forced it open and it exploded! There was chicken paprikas all over the walls and on the ceiling. It took us hours to clean up and I was told to get a girlfriend to cook for me. I took this advice to heart so I went to the nearby hospital where there were many pretty nurses. I found a delightful nurse, Joyce and we dated for quite a while. Soon another bachelor got married and Peter Kolbusz, my friend joined us at the townhouse.

Several of us took a trip to Belgium to visit the World Fair and then another one to Paris. We got into a taxi and told the driver we want to see something typical for Paris. The driver took us to a theatre with plush seats and plenty of elbow room, but without a screen. We were really confused. After a while, the lights went out and we noticed that there was a window on the floor in front of every seat. We were looking down into a well-lighted living room. After a while a man and a woman came into the room, had some drinks, then the woman went out and came back naked, but on roller skates! Well… I guess it served me right for doubting my friend!

When I got back to England, I bought an old Humber sedan from the landlord at Maida Vale. It was big but with a small engine. Our third trip was to Italy in the Humber. It took us around in Rome and up to Venice, except in Florence it broke down. The head gasket was blown. Nobody had parts for an old English car in Florence and we could not afford to linger around or leave the car there. We convinced a garage to help us, where I fashioned a head gasket out of a sheet of softened copper and away we went.

I got a job with a Hungarian engineer, who invented a method of 'globulizing' fly ash. Fly ash is the result of burning coal in a furnace. Since the coal always contains a bit of non-combustible material, the unburnt part becomes dust referred to as fly ash. Power stations spent money to have the fly ash transported by trucks to a disposal site. When they were able to give the fly ash away for free, the power companies were happy to be rid of it without the extra cost. The Hungarian engineer had a great idea to form globules from the ash, which was done by molding or melting the dust particles together into a useable form, usually balls.

There was demand for these balls because they did not burn. My job was to design the machines that globulized the fly ash. We were successful and today there are artificial roof tiles on the market, which look like Spanish tiles, made from fly ash. They do not burn and are much lighter and cheaper than Spanish roof tiles.

I met another Hungarian refugee who wanted to sell his car, a 1924 Standard 18. I bought it from him for 20 pounds. I took it home and checked the water and oil in the engine. There was none so I added water to the radiator. It took a lot of water and after a while, I notice I was standing in a puddle. All the water I poured in had leaked out at the bottom.

I went back to the seller and told him what happened. He got upset and told me I should have known the car needed gasoline to run, not water! It turned out he never added water to the car, yet it ran for years. Of course, there was no oil in it either. When I filled the oil reservoir, it also poured out and puddled under the car. But the car ran, not very fast, but it actually ran and I drove it for over a year without any oil and water. It was also missing the driver's side running board, the step that can be used to get into the car, so I fashioned one out of a scrap diamond plate.

The running board was so heavy that it weighed the car down on the driver's side. There was also no window glass on the passenger side or on the sunroof. My girlfriend carried an umbrella while in the car whenever we went to the ocean. When we got to an incline, the car only had enough power to go uphill in reverse. We would have to turn the car around and go up the hill backward. That was truly a memorable car, but it got me around and that was all I needed it to do.

Later in 1957, I got a very good job with the prestigious Eubank and Partners engineering firm that was in the process of designing a nuclear power station. I was involved in working on the design of the Wilmington B power station. The company's offices were directly across from the Queen's Castle and from my office I could see into the castle's rooms.

The firm was very formal. Every engineer wore a dark-blue suit. One day I went to work in a dark-brown suit. Mr. Eubank personally came down from his office to send me home to change because he did not like my suit.

Everything was tightly scheduled. The office ran according to plan. The secretaries arrived at 8 a.m., the engineers at 9 am. At 9:30 the secretaries had breakfast tea, followed by the engineers who had their tea at 10:30 am. Next, the secretaries had lunch at 12 noon, followed by the engineers, who had lunch at one. When we returned from lunch at 2 pm, the secretaries had afternoon tea at 2:30, followed by the engineer's afternoon tea at 3:30. At 4:30 the secretaries went home and at 5 p.m. we went home. How we accomplished anything was a miracle!

Late in 1958, I received a letter from the National Academy of Sciences of United States of America informing me President Eisenhower instructed them to choose five nuclear engineers to be brought into the USA and I was selected. I was told to go to the US Embassy, which I did and to my surprise, I was allowed to enter. Previously I had been denied entry – several times. After being interrogated, I was asked to fill out a 63-page questionnaire. They knew I was a member of a communist scout group in Hungary and thankfully they agreed that given the time and place, being in that scout group was unavoidable if I wanted to get a degree.

I kept a copy of my answers to the interrogation in case I needed them later. Soon I was summoned to the embassy again and asked to fill out the exact same questionnaire again. The notes I kept of my answers came very handy. By then the communists found out that the United States wanted me, so *they* tried to get me also.

This all happened when I was living with the four bachelors on Molineou Street in London. A man and woman came looking for me, claiming to be my friends, and insisted on talking to me. One of my roommates, a Swiss-born patent attorney, was sick that day, so he remained home. Luckily, my roommates were all warned by the English Secret Service that the communists may try to locate me. The Swiss roommate was aware what might happen, so he said that I was not at home and would not give them any more information.

When the man and woman finally left, my roommate called me. I was working at Eubank and Partners, so I called the number the American Embassy gave me in case something happened, I don't remember if it was National Security Agency (NSA) or the Central Intelligence Agency (CIA), but whoever it was, called their contact at Scotland Yard. They investigated and found there was a Hungarian bookstore in London serving as a front for a communist group that was trying to stop me. The bookstore was legitimate, but it was also a secret headquarters for the communist group who worked out of the business. They could read all the newspaper stories there to stay informed. I was also told that the Hungarian communist government found my father, arrested and beat him.

I was given approval to immigrate to America as part of a special quota. To accept the offer and move to the United States, I had to sell everything that I could not carry within a week.

I had been trying for two years to immigrate and wanted to go. However, I had a lot to do in a very little amount of time to be ready for the move. One day I was driving the old Standard 18 around Piccadilly Circus and a bobby gave me a ticket for 20 pounds, which had to be paid right there. I told him he could have the car instead. He was speechless but nevertheless he took the car. I never learned what happened to the car, but it was one less thing I had to deal with. I was able to walk away and leave England. I was given free passage on the last trip of the Libertee, a German Ocean liner, which was scrapped upon arrival in New York.

Chapter 11:
Arriving in America

I was invited to America by the President of the United States, Dwight Eisenhower, by way of the National Science Academy. This was a great honor and only a few people were chosen to participate in this special program.

However, when I arrived, two men from NSA greeted me at the port of New York. They had very bad news for me. My father had been arrested by the communists and they were torturing him, trying to force him to write me and convince me to return to Hungary. He refused and the NSA representatives were concerned that if I followed through and worked on nuclear power, the communist might kill my father. The NSA assured me there were efforts underway to get my father out of prison, but they told me those would take time. I requested that they get me another job which, sadly, they were unable to do. Wanting to be helpful, they referred me to an organization responsible for helping immigrants called 'Assistance to Immigrants in the Profession'.

The organization got me several temporary jobs, like cleaning offices for Mattel and other similar jobs. When I had work, I slept at the YMCA for $2 and days, when there was no work, I slept in Central Park. I spent a lot of time worrying about my father and my family back home, wondering what was happening to them. I did not know if my father was alive or dead.

My friend, Peter Grosz, wanted me to travel to Detroit, where he was working at that time and loaned me money to get there. He suggested that I apply for a job he heard was open with General

Motors to design windshield wipers. I applied but was dismissed by a woman at the desk accepting applications, because I had never designed windshield wipers before.

My life-long friend, Peter, in New York

I asked her how difficult could it be to design a windshield wiper for someone with an advanced engineering degree? I could not understand how they were going to find somebody who designed windshield wipers, unless they took them from Ford or Chrysler. The woman told me that she was instructed to simply hire an experienced windshield wiper designer so I was out of luck.

Soon I met a nice lady at the desk of *Assistance to Immigrants in the Profession.* I bought her dinner with the last of my money and we became friends and I ended up staying with her for a while. I felt it necessary to have transportation so that I could apply for jobs outside of New York and she helped me get a small car, a Fiat sedan. I found ways to attend various conventions, even though I was not invited. I went from room to room meeting people and offering my services.

At one convention I attended for engineers, I met a Hungarian engineer working for Pittsburgh Plate Glass Company Research Center in Pittsburgh. He arranged for an interview for me at PPG. I drove the Fiat from New York to Pittsburgh for the interview. Driving back via the Pennsylvania Turnpike, the weather was balmy and I only had a light jacket with me. The Turnpike runs through the Appalachian Mountains in the center of Pennsylvania, tunneling through the mountainous part of the road.

When I got through the tunnel, I was confronted with a severe snow storm on the east side of the mountain. I witnessed a large Ford sedan carrying six passengers get blown off the road and into a ditch upon exiting the tunnel. All of the passengers got thrown out of the car and sadly none survived. In 1958 there were no seatbelts in cars and there was no power steering. Suddenly, slightly scared, and realizing I could die in this severe storm I pushed myself into the seat as much as I could, turned off the engine and let the car drift down the hill. I had to keep moving so I went on being as careful as I could in that small car.

The Fiat was blown towards the ditch and steering was ineffective. There was nothing I could do. The car rolled over one-and-a-half times ending up on its side in the ditch. All of the windows were shattered. The engine had been pushed back next to me in the car seat and I was covered with blood.

After a while, I realized I wasn't injured and I had only bitten my tongue, which was the source of the blood. But now I was freezing because the snow was still blowing very hard. The Highway Patrol arrived soon but told me I had to wait because they were busy trying to help the people thrown out of the Ford. A nice couple drove by slowly and gave me a ride to their home, which was nearby. I spent the night there and they loaned me money to travel by bus to New York. The insurance company had the Fiat rebuilt, but I didn't trust it anymore. I drove it for awhile until I had enough money to buy another one.

One good thing did come out of that entire ordeal. At the Physicist Convention in Manhattan in 1958, I was offered the position of Research Engineer at PPG. I took the position and moved to Pittsburgh. I was hired to develop a tool for bending glass for rear windows in cars like the Mercury sedan and others. The plate glass sections were positioned on a fixture, which moved on a conveyor system through a long furnace, called a 'Lehrer'. The glass was heated by radiant burners as it moved. Once the plates got warm, they sagged and bent more or less to the desired shape.

My task was to adjust the heat of the burners and contour of the supporting structure, in order to bend the plate. Many plates broke during experimentation while finding the right contours. I was told by my department manager to break at least 60 plates a day to meet my quota. This manager was proud to have started as a janitor and achieve promotion to manager without getting any sort of degree. He was promoted to manager because he was a union member and had been employed there for so long.

PPG was having trouble with the trade union, which defined a day's work was accomplished, when a fixed number of glass plates went through the furnace. Since many plates broke half way through the furnace, the worker at the front of the Lehrer was finished when he fed in the specified number of plates, but the workers at the other end still did not have enough plates to meet their quota.

PPG had to pay overtime to the workers at the front end of the Lehrer to keep supplying plates until the workers at the back end had enough pieces to meet their quota. That was a crazy and an expensive way to solve the problem. PPG was unable to negotiate an acceptable contract with the union, so their solution was to build another factory in another state and lay everybody off in Pittsburgh. Friday was payday and this particular Friday there were pink slips in the pay envelopes. I remember that was a wild Friday afternoon.

A competing company in England developed a method to bend the side windows of cars, which, until then, had always been flat. I had solved several problems of bending the back windows, so I was given the task to develop a different method than our competitor used to bend the glass, but achieve the same result. I eventually came up with a way.

To bend the glass I made two molds, one was convex and the other concave at the same curvature. The soft glass was poured into the molds, which pressed the glass into the desired curved shape. The glass was placed on a surface and heated with radiant burners to soften it to the appropriate temperature. If that temperature was not achieved, the window would not curve and it would shatter. PPG patented the method and today, most cars have bent side windows. The English competitor eventually filed an international law suit and after many months, it was decided that PPG only could manufacture curved windows in the United States.

The next task I had there was to work on 'curtain walls', frameless windows, which cover the entire outside wall of large buildings. The first such curtain wall was installed in a hotel in Philadelphia. It soon crumbled. My task was to analyze what destroyed that curtain wall and devise a solution to eliminate the problem.

It was not a difficult task. I determined that the pressure differences between the inside and the outside of the building, created by the blowing wind, destroyed the wall. The solution that I recommended was to place small holes across the frame to equalize the inside and outside pressure. I know of no curtain walls that have fallen since that solution was implemented.

Around that time, I saw a Jaguar XK140MC sport car advertised for sale in Pittsburgh. It was more expensive than what I could afford, but I asked to drive it around just for fun. To my surprise, the owner really wanted to get rid of the car because his young son was reckless and the man was concerned for his son's safety. The owner not only reduced his asking price, he financed the Jaguar for me making the purchase possible. I was meant to have this car!

It was a fast car for its time — except in the rain because when it rained, the engine simply stopped. I figured out that the distributor was not watertight; it was only able to handle one rain-induced puddle.

I worked with an engineer who dated a very pretty girl named Sally, who invited me to meet her sister, Joyce. I found out that Joyce was ready to find a partner, so we began dating and we fell in love.

Sally was young and adventurous. One time her parents went on a trip to South America and took Sally with them. She met someone there who really fell in love with her, even though Sally was only 16 years-old. After they returned home, the man came to Pittsburgh and asked Sally to meet him downtown. Her parents were very upset, but neither of them was willing to stop her, so they asked me to go after Sally and bring her home which I did.

*   *   *   *

Once I drove to New York with my good friend Peter Grosz in the Jaguar and had a good time going about 120 mph on the Pennsylvania turnpike. We realized the ticket we got when entering the turnpike had the time stamped on it so we decided that we should not exit too early or we might get an expensive speeding ticket. To kill time, we decided to stop for a bite to eat, but had to visit the restroom first. We weren't paying attention and accidentally went into the ladies' room. When we realized our mistake, we quickly turned around and found the men's room, but a woman standing in line for the bathroom with several daughters saw us coming out of the ladies' room and assumed they were at the wrong door. The woman and her family moved to the other door, which *was* the men's room, causing quite a bit of confusion for a little while. In the end, we all took care of our business in the proper place.

When Peter and I arrived in Manhattan and entered the tunnel, there was considerable congestion there, so we had to slow down. The engine's cooling system wasn't able to cool things down fast enough after driving at 120 mph, so in the slow tunnel traffic, the engine overheated. We had no alternative, but to stop for a while and let the engine cool down. Soon the New York Police pulled up and ordered us to get going so the traffic could move along. We argued with the policeman long enough for the engine to cool down a bit and off we went.

The Jag was the first car ever produced with a telescoping steering column – the kind that you can push in and pull out. I spontaneously demonstrated this feature to my future wife, Joyce, while driving through a tunnel in Pittsburgh. I pulled the steering wheel towards myself when unexpectedly it came off the steering column. I handed the wheel to Joyce and told her to steer for a while. She *screamed* nonstop so, I had to re-install the wheel and drive.

I had so many adventures in that car. When I got married and had to get a blood test for the marriage license, the nurse was not very good. She poked so many holes into my arm that I got rather upset and when I got back into the car, I let the clutch out too fast and the rear axle fell out. The torque tore the axle right off the semi-elliptic springs that held it in place. Even with that, it was a spectacular car! It was around that time that the NSA notified me that my father was out of prison, which meant that I was free to work on a nuclear power, fulfilling my purpose in America.

Chapter 12:

My Work On the Hubble Telescope

I was hired by the Copes Vulcan Division in Erie, Pennsylvania in 1959 to work on the Polaris nuclear submarine. My task was to develop a valve that could dump the radioactive cooling water in case of emergency. Water is used to cool the nuclear reactor that powers the submarines, resulting in radioactive water. If the submarine was damaged or had a mechanical failure, the radioactive water had to be removed from the vessel.

The problem I had to solve happened when a submarine ran deeper than the 'critical depth' when water could no longer be dumped into the sea. The reason is because the pressure of the ocean at that critical depth is higher than the pressure of the cooling water that had to be removed from the sub. The valve used to move the radioactive water had to have built-in pressure sensor and redirect the flow to a holding tank when the outside water pressure was too high. It was a complex valve and I had to know the depth that these submarines could go, which was critical to their success in war and a highly guarded secret.

I was given a Royal McBee computer to do the computations. Royal McBee was a division of Royal Typewriter Company, but typewriters were not yet a common item in every office. The Royal McBee stored data on a revolving drum, which held only 64 kbits of data. The computer used perforated tapes, like a telegraph machine, for data entry. Output was also on a punched tape. This made for a very slow and clumsy process. It was necessary to break the calculations, into segments. After solving equations for the first segment of a program, the punched tape output produced from that step had to be entered into the punched tape reader in order to perform the next segment of the calculation.

After watching the machine work all night many times, I had a brainstorm. I fed the beginning of the output tape into the input tape reader and went home to sleep. I expected a solution to be ready the next morning, but I failed to consider the overnight cleaning crew. They saw all of that paper tape on the floor and cleaned it up! All my work was lost.

It was such a disappointment I had to stay many nights to make up for that error in judgment, just to finish the design. Finally, I completed my task and when I was done, I knew it was the perfect solution.

I decided to go back to school to get my PhD, so I enrolled at the University of Pittsburgh through a Westinghouse sponsored program. I was lucky: my father was able to mail my diploma from the Technical University of Budapest. The diploma was accepted as on-par with a Master's Degree, so I was admitted to the PhD program. I worked insane hours and rarely slept.

I found out after getting married, Joyce was on the "rebound" from a previous boyfriend, as she put it. We agreed that Joyce would complete her studies before we had children, but soon, in 1960, she was pregnant with my son, Paul.

To my distress, Paul was a breach baby and Joyce had to have a Caesarean section. I had to give my consent for the operation, but in Hungary that procedure carried a huge risk, so I called and requested the advice of Joyce's father, who was a pharmacist and knew many doctors. He assured me the procedure was safe, but due to the delay caused by my concern and need to research, Joyce was rushed into the operating room and the Caesarean section was performed at the last minute before Paul was too far into the birth canal. Thankfully, everything turned out well.

After getting married, my father-in-law gave my wife a Plymouth Fury as a wedding present. Joyce drove it all summer, but when snow fell in Pittsburgh, the car could not even get out of the garage. The following summer it drove just fine until the steering rod broke at an intersection. One front wheel was pointing to the left, the other to the right.

That car was handy transportation for Joyce for a while anyway. When Paul was born, we traded my Jaguar for a Volvo sedan. It was much slower, but the reliability was outstanding. It never broke down, but I finally got bored with it and sold it some years later.

My advisor at the University was the Chief Engineer at J.W. Fecker, a company in Pittsburgh. Fecker was the second most recognized manufacturer of astronomical telescopes at the time. The company had a contract with NASA to work on the development of a space telescope. That research was the foundation for the Hubble Telescope.

In 1960, the professor invited me to join him at Fecker to work on the space telescope and I worked at J.W. Fecker for two years. I knew this was an amazing opportunity, not only for my career but also to be on the forefront of science. This was the type of thing I had been dreaming about my entire life, but little did I think I would be able to work on something as incredible as the Hubble Telescope.

The Assembly Tower for the Hubble Telescope

The first task I had at Fecker was to select the right material for the primary mirror of the Hubble space telescope. It had to be light, it had to distort as little as possible due to large changes in temperature, it had to be ground and polished, and the material had to withstand the 'g' forces encountered during launch. I considered conventional quartz, but it was too heavy for space. I also tried aluminum, beryllium, and titanium. I made several mirrors about 2 feet in diameter out of different materials to test them.

Beryllium was the most suitable, but it cracked during machining and the crack propagated uncontrollably. Even with that, beryllium was the final choice due to its *strength-to-weight* ratio. A great deal of development was required to achieve the desired characteristics of the mirror. Thanks, in part to my efforts, space mirrors are still being built from beryllium.

Next, we built a small test mirror. It was small compared to the Hubble telescope's primary mirror, but it was large enough to test its deformation at temperatures prevailing in space. We installed it in a cold room at NASA Goddard in Maryland. The room was so cold that I had to wear two Eskimo suits, one on top of the other, to enter the chamber for 30 minutes. I could not re-enter again for another four hours. In order to perform the extreme accuracy optical tests, it was difficult to see clearly through the goggles I had to wear. One time I took the goggles off to complete the test and the skin around my eye immediately froze to the instrument.

Fecker also built a space simulation laboratory at United Aircraft. United Aircraft was formed in 1929 when Boeing and Pratt and Whitney merged the aviation interests in their companies, creating this new company to serve all areas of aviation, both civil and military. A Swiss-born engineer oversaw the Fecker project at United Aircraft. The instrumentation of the spacecraft to be tested was mounted on a steel plate that was to be supported on a large steel ball allowing it to move freely in all directions. In turn, the steel ball was to be supported on a shaft that would be threaded into the ball.

When the ball was threaded onto the shaft halfway in, it galled and jammed due to friction. Several days were spent, without success, trying to thread it all the way in or unthread and remove it. It was impossible to grab the ball with a strong tool without damaging it.

I was asked to do something to correct the problem. The entire project was about to fail because of this one unexpected situation. After I arrived and thought the problem for a while, I took the leather belt that was holding up my trousers and wrapped it around the ball. I thought this would allow me to hold the ball perfectly still so it would tighten on the shaft as we rotated the ball, but I did not have enough strength. As I struggled with this problem, many spectators gathered around watching the attempts to secure the ball to the shaft.

I shouted at one man standing by 'Don't just watch me, get a 4x4!' He did as I asked, and I nailed the 4x4 wooden beam to the free end of my belt and, with the help of that same man, managed to unscrew the ball. Next, I lubricated the threads of the shaft and successfully installed the ball on the shaft. The next day I was told to go up to the office of the President of United Aircraft. It turns out that the President was the man I had shouted at! He had come down to watch our efforts because he was concerned that NASA would cancel our contract, but thankfully, he was quite pleased with the result and invited me to his office to thank me personally.

Chapter 13:
My Presidential Commendation at NASA

My daughter Renee was born in 1962, like her brother Paul through a Caesarean section. Renee was extremely allergic, which we discovered when she stopped breathing when she was two-years-old. One day she could not breathe so I rushed her to the Pittsburgh Children's Hospital emergency room at about 7:30 a.m. Traffic in Pittsburgh was very bad, but I couldn't wait for an ambulance, so I drove, flashing my lights, slamming on my brakes, and honking my horn, while going the wrong way on a one-way street. I was in such a blind panic I hardly even thought about what I was doing. I was willing to risk everything to keep my daughter alive.

The police, instead of pulling me over, understood there was something wrong, so they stopped traffic for me. When I arrived at the hospital I had no brakes left. Thankfully, the parking lot was tilted downhill toward the hospital so I just rammed the car into the wall. I picked Renee up and ran her into the emergency room.

Unfortunately, Pittsburgh Children's was a terrible hospital. The doctors and nurses did all kinds of things to her; however, she would not stop screaming. She was put in a restraining jacket like mental patients wear but she still screamed. Soon I noticed that she had stopped breathing again, so I ran into the corridor yelling for help. An Indian doctor came over and took one look at her, cut the restraint jacket off and screamed for some assistance. There weren't any nurses, aids or attendants around when he said he had to perform a tracheotomy on her. He asked if I had a knife on me. I didn't have a knife but did I have a ballpoint pen, which I gave him. I held Renee in my arms and the doctor, who was very good, performed the tracheotomy using my ballpoint pen.

I was concerned that Renee was going to die. I pictured how devastated Joyce would be. But miraculously, Renee started to breathe again. The doctor then used sedatives and tranquilizers, which put her in a drug-induced coma. For nine days she was under but finally came out of it very slowly. The important thing is that she regained consciousness.

At the time, our home was a very small house and we didn't have an air conditioner or ventilation. The doctor said she was very allergic to dust, so we had to get rid of everything that could hold dust, like curtains, carpets, and all soft surfaces. She was particularly allergic to Sisal and after she had several more asthma attacks, I took a knife and cut open her mattress. As I suspected, it was all full of Sisal. I tried to buy a foam rubber mattress, but it turned out that every foam rubber mattress was wrapped in Sisal. I kept researching and eventually found a mattress manufacturer and had them make a mattress without the Sisal cover. We also had to seal every door, every window.

In the winter, the furnace blew hot air into the house which might contain allergens that would cause another asthma attack. While working in a power station, I learned about electrostatic precipitators, used by the power stations to clean the air. Electrostatic precipitators electrically charge any dust in section one, and in section two there are highly charged electromagnets that attract the charged dust particles and capture them. It is an exceptionally high-quality air cleaner that gets the contamination in the air down to no more than two or three microns, which can only be done with electrostatically.

There was no electrostatic precipitator available for homes in 1964, but I got one from a power station, which was being replaced with a better one. I repaired the discarded industrial precipitator and put it into the air duct. The furnace was blowing air into the precipitator and then blowing it into the house. That helped Renee a little bit, but her asthma was a constant problem.

My daughter Rene

Around this time, Fecker was building extremely precise gyro test tables. Gyros are the instruments used to guide airplanes by displaying to the pilot the direction the plane is flying. The test tables calibrated the gyros for the cockpit. Fecker received a contract from Hughes Aircraft to build three master test tables to calibrate the gyro test tables. These 'master' tables had extreme accuracy and I was put in charge of the project. Eventually, the US Air Force, Germany, and Italy each bought a master table. The most accurate was the USAF unit installed in Toledo Ohio. I had to install it underground on a very large pendulum to ensure that it was isolated from vibration and weather changes.

One day, while installing a gyro test table at Hughes in El Segundo, California, my attention was diverted when everybody ran to the windows. I asked what was happening and was told that Mr.

Hughes was coming. That did no sound unusual for me since Mr. Hughes owned the company. However, I was told that Mr. Hughes *never* came by. When he arrived, he did not get out of his limousine, but simply lowered the window and spoke to a corporate officer, who was waiting for his arrival. The next day I could not work because everything was being painted green. I mean everything – walls, floors, chairs, tables, everything. I was told Mr. Hughes had told them to paint, so they did.

Next, J.W. Fecker received a contract to build a Space Simulator at NASA Ames in the San Francisco Peninsula. I was put in charge of that project which was completed successfully and on time. I received a presidential commendation around 1971. Every NASA spacecraft's controls were tested there for decades.

The entire laboratory was in a spherical vacuum chamber over 20 feet in diameter. It rested on a very large eight-foot-deep reinforced concrete block slab to isolate it from ground vibrations. Unfortunately, the subcontractor poured the concrete about four feet north of where it was supposed to be. Consequently, the slab had to be extended four feet to the south to rectify the problem and the extension had to be stable like the original and seamless in its construction.

If that wasn't bad enough, the subcontractor had a group of very careless electrical technicians working on the project, who dropped tools, parts and other items from the scaffolds they were working on. We all knew not to be near or under the scaffolds they worked on. There were also two brothers working on details of the building construction. They were the most careful and considerate people I ever met. Sadly, one day, as they were preparing to install railing on an observer's balcony, one brother lost his balance and fell. The other brother reached for him, trying to prevent him from falling off. He managed to grab his brother but was pulled off the balcony with his brother. They both fell over 20 feet onto the concrete floor below. One brother died instantly, the other brother sustained brain damage that left him a vegetable for the rest of his life. That was a tragic event that should not have happened.

Another event involved my son, Paul, who was in elementary school. Outside of the Space Simulator building, engineers were developing the controls for a hovercraft. Today, the antique hovercraft has evolved to what we call a helicopter, but back then it was a very exciting innovation. I took my son so he could observe the difficulties pilots have controlling aircraft.

The next day in school, he told the other children about what he had seen at NASA. When his teacher heard the story, Paul was ordered to retract his lies, but he insisted that he was not lying and he was taken to the principal's office. The principal, in turn, called me and told me to take my lying son home. I went to see the principal and explained that Paul was not lying. I told him that NASA is full of new, exciting developments that an average person cannot even imagine. I wanted to take the principal in to see what I was talking about, but he didn't have clearance, so I could not.

My father, mother, my wife, Joyce, and my Son Paul around 1971

While the Space Simulator was being built, I got involved with the predecessor of the Hubble space telescope. NASA gutted the cargo bay of a DC-8 cargo plane and installed a 36" telescope looking out sideways. It was placed to look out at the cargo door. The idea was to prove that at high altitude the telescope had a much better view than at ground level since the image is not distorted by air full of moisture and other contaminants. The experiment was a success and NASA got funding for the Hubble telescope. Due to my work on this project, I was later hired to design the suspension system of the primary mirror of the Hubble Space Telescope to achieve $1/20^{th}$ wavelength accuracy in space after launch. This design was the subject of my PhD dissertation, entitled "Suspension of Elastic Plates on Multiple Points on Multiple Concentric Circles".

Post Script

Although my life wasn't an easy one, I made sure to have fun along the way and never let anything stop me. Ever since I was 12 years old, I've wanted to move to the United States. I always knew my future lay in this wonderful country where I would able to use my skills, if I had the opportunity. I will always be grateful I was able to escape communism and come to America and accomplish so much.

It was worth fighting through all the difficult times to finally arrive in the United States, and settle down and be able to work in some amazing companies.

In 1968 I became Chief Engineer for Fairchild Camera Space and Defence Vision, and in 1974 I started and managed several companies with my friend Peter Grosz. I was president of Renmark Pacific Corporation, GRW, and Kinetron.

The States has always been a country of exploration and in some small way I was able to be a part of it. I helped build the Satellite Attitude Control Space Simulator for NASA. Probably the pinnacle of my achievement was the Assembly Tower for the Hubble Telescope, one of the most versatile and well-known telescopes ever built.

As an engineer and builder, I was always fascinated with creating new things. Through my long career I was able to patent a hydraulic jacking system that raised the Freemont Street Bridge in one piece. I built an air cargo handling and weighing system for the US Air Force and major airlines. I also created a latch system for tug boats and barges. I am grateful I could contribute to America in many ways through my inventions.

As part of my fascination with the way things worked, I had a lifelong love affair with cars. I had many amazing vehicles which I would often rebuild and race.

One of the more memorable cars I bought was a partially dismantled Alfa Romeo Sprint Special. The seller intended to rebuild the engine, but could not figure out how to assemble it. It took me a while to put it all together and install it in the car.

However, a few minutes after I started the car, the engine failed. I took it apart, and again rebuilt it, installed it, but it failed in less than five minutes. I rebuilt it a third time and finally figured out one of the rubber hoses I connected to the engine was in the wrong place.

After that it ran well. I raced it at a track at an abandoned airport north of San Francisco. However, the engine only lasted about two races, before I had to rebuild it again. It became a routine effort after a while. I had all the special tools and spare parts imported from Italy. It had two carburetors that, amazingly, had to be synchronized by sticking rubber hoses in my ears and listening to the whistle. When they were in tune it was ready to go. I had many adventures with my cars and I enjoyed all of them.

Bonnie and I Hosting a formal party in 2007, celebrating my 75th birthday

Unfortunately, Joyce and I divorced and in 1995, but I got remarried in 2002 to Bonnie, an amazing woman and the love of my life. I was very sad when, unfortunately, she passed away in 2013.

I now have five grandchildren and three great-grandchildren. I am also still in touch with Bonnie's children and we see each other frequently.

I achieved a satisfying retirement in Sherman Oaks, California but am still very active and enjoy life. I now fill up my time with my current squeeze Margie, tennis, and pet projects.

Having Fun with Margie

Happily Enjoying Retirement

Made in the USA
San Bernardino, CA
12 May 2020

71477170R00053